2014

to George
xx

A wee surpuse
jist for you!
? ? ?

BLOODY S

HIST(

C000246498

ABERDEEN

BLOODY SCOTTISH HISTORY

HISTORY

ABERDEEN

ELMA MCMENEMY

The
History
Press

In memory of my Auntie Anne,
Annie Hutton Numbers, MA, BSc, PhD, 1897–1988,
one of the 'spinster generation'.

Without her unfailing guidance and encouragement in my early life
I would have achieved very little.

First published in 2014

The History Press
The Mill, Brimscombe Port
Stroud, Gloucestershire, GL5 2QG
www.thehistorypress.co.uk

ISBN 978 0 7524 8740 3

Typesetting and origination by The History Press
Printed in Great Britain

CONTENTS

ACKNOWLEDGEMENTS

I **HAVE REALLY** enjoyed writing this, have learned a huge amount and have been amazed and humbled by the ready assistance offered by so many people – but then, Aberdeen is that sort of place.

I first mentioned the book at a meeting of the Aberdeen City and Shire Ancestral Tourism Partnership and was instantly given ideas and offers of help. Thanks to all of you, in particular Phil Astley, Aberdeen City Archivist; Fiona Watson, Archivist to NHS Grampian; Jean Shirer of Aberdeen & NE Scotland Family History Society; and Andrew MacGregor, Deputy Archivist, University of Aberdeen Library, Special Collections and Museums. John Edwards, at that time Head of Collections, Aberdeen City Museums and Galleries, ensured his enthusiastic staff helped however they could: Dr Christopher P. Croly, Aberdeen City Historian, readily shared his own carefully researched information – I couldn't have done this without your help! Meredith Greiling, Curator of Maritime History; Judith Stones, Lead Curator, Local History and Archaeology; and Jenny Brown, Curator, Industry, also helped in different ways. Jesper Ericsson, Curator of The Gordon Highlanders Museum, was an absolute star, sharing information, providing illustrations and checking details for three chapters in no time flat.

Organisations, business acquaintances, colleagues, friends and family also helped with particular chapters, including Historic Scotland; Blairs Museum Trust; Captain Daniel Stroud and Dianne Insh of Aberdeen Harbour Board; Dr Arthur Winfield of The Open Space Trust; Jake Molloy of the RMT union representing offshore workers; Regina Erich; Blue Badge Guide Pam Wells; and Bev Clarke, serial ancestral visitor, living in Tasmania but also firmly rooted in north east Scotland, who happily allowed me to use some of her painstaking family research. My sister, Lorna Numbers, RRC (Colonel ret'd QARANC), explained with her usual clarity points of medical and military detail, while my niece Rachael McMenemy refreshed my memory on Shakespeare's *Macbeth*.

Several people preferred not to be named, but I certainly could not have done this without their support. A *special* retired soldier who, together with his father-in-law, prevented potential military combat faux pas; two helicopter pilots, one retired, the other still flying enthusiastically offshore; and an amazing friend who patiently read and re-read every word, checked details and corrected grammar, punctuation and ambiguities. You all know who you are – thank you!

To Cate Ludlow of The History Press, thank you for asking me, and for your unfailing support, patience and flexibility.

Sincere thanks to my husband Brian for his encouragement, wielding his teacher's red pen as required and for countless cups of coffee, glasses of wine, the occasional inspirational malt whisky and for understanding when so often I couldn't do other things; apologies for trying to fit too much work into too few hours – again! And finally, hugs to my two lovely Deerhounds Sula and Gigha – stress-busters extraordinaires.

Any mistakes are, of course, my own.

INTRODUCTION

THE ABERDEEN WE know today evolved from two distinct settlements surrounded by small villages, now all incorporated into the city. The two main settlements were very different.

To the north, by the River Don, a town grew up which we now call Old Aberdeen; this developed as a centre for Christianity and learning. St Machar, a disciple of St Columba, brought Christianity here about the year AD 580. Tradition tells that Columba told Machar to travel from Iona across Scotland until he came to a place near the sea and close to a river which flowed in the shape of a bishop's staff. Certainly, the place where he chose to settle and build his simple church was less than a mile from the North Sea and on land close to the River Don, where he is believed to have performed baptisms. Today, the Cathedral Church of St Machar stands on the same site. One of the world's oldest granite cathedrals, most of the present building dates from the 1300s and early 1400s. It was here in Old Aberdeen, in 1495, that Bishop William Elphinstone founded a university for the north of Scotland. King's College, named after King James IV who supported the university financially, was an important part of what became a prosperous burgh. Today, it is the main campus for the University of Aberdeen, with 500-year-old King's College Chapel very much at its heart.

Meanwhile, to the south, the estuary of the River Dee provided a natural harbour. In 1136, King David I granted

Cathedral Church of St Machar, Old Aberdeen. (Author's collection)

ROYAL THIEVERY!

Around 450 years ago, with the future King James VI (later James I of England) still an infant, the Regent, the Earl of Moray, sent his henchmen to Old Aberdeen. Their instructions were to take the lead from the roof of the old Roman Catholic St Machar's Cathedral, then disused and neglected. The Regent planned to sell the lead to raise funds to pay his army. His men took not only the lead but also the huge bronze bells from the great central tower. All this booty was carried to Aberdeen Harbour and loaded onto a ship. But no sooner had the vessel sailed, than a huge storm blew up and the ship sank to the bottom of Aberdeen Bay. It is said it still lies there today with its cargo intact because it rests at the outflow of the city's old Victorian sewage system!

the bishops and clergy of Old Aberdeen the right to demand dues or taxes from the ships using the harbour. The port ensured the town's growth and prosperity and attracted merchants, traders and shipbuilders and also Vikings, pirates – and the English! It was here in this merchant and trading town that Aberdeen's second university was founded in 1593. Named Marischal (say it 'marshall') College after its founder George Keith, the Earl Marischal of Scotland, it was a Protestant rival for the Catholic King's College in Old Aberdeen. For centuries, Aberdonians have been proud to boast that their city had two universities at a time when there were only two in the whole of England, at Oxford and Cambridge, albeit each had several colleges.

Aberdeen benefited greatly from its natural resources – fish from the sea and rivers, produce from its hinterland and high-quality granite. This fine silver stone was used not only for buildings, bridges and mansions throughout the city, the base of the famous Bell Rock Lighthouse and the piers of the Forth Rail Bridge, but was also sent farther afield – to London for the Embankment, Waterloo Bridge and the Cenotaph, and to Paris for L'Opéra.

'Town', the trading port, and 'Gown', the University and Old Aberdeen, developed an even closer relationship. First, in 1860, the two universities united to form the University of Aberdeen, then in 1891 Old Aberdeen and New Aberdeen came together under one Town Council. Old Aberdeen's beautiful Georgian Town House was no longer needed.

Like many other British cities, as Aberdeen expanded it absorbed nearby villages, including Woodside, Fittie (sometimes called Footdee), Ferryhill and more recently Cove Bay, Bucksburn, Dyce, Cults and Culter. Unlike most other cities, however, Aberdeen has always been inextricably linked to its hinterland, not only the Aberdeenshire of old but also the other counties which now make up the administrative area of Aberdeenshire – the Mearns/Kincardineshire, Buchan and Banffshire. During the 1860s and '70s, the rebuilding of the Town House in New Aberdeen included a shared meeting hall. Known as the

Town and County Hall, this was used both by Aberdeen Town Council and Aberdeen County Council. This shared facility was the result of a plan to save money – perhaps it was one of many things which gave rise to the stories about Aberdonians being mean?

During the two world wars, Aberdeen, its important harbour, shipyards and engineering works were targets for enemy attack. Today the city is of vital importance to the offshore oil and gas industry. Aberdeen Harbour Board, the UK's oldest business, founded in 1136, has invested heavily to create a world-class port which supports and supplies offshore rigs and platforms in the North Sea and beyond. This, together with investments by the City Council, Aberdeen International Airport, the University of Aberdeen and The Robert Gordon University, has encouraged global oil and gas companies to make Aberdeen their North Sea base. As a result, Aberdeen is now known as Europe's Offshore Oil Capital.

The chapters which follow can only scratch the surface of the history of this proud city. Aberdeen has long been a city of commerce and trade but, with its hinterland, it has seen more than its fair share of bloodshed, intrigue and tales of heroism and derring-do. Illustrations include present-day photographs of some of the locations mentioned. Open your eyes when you explore Aberdeen City and Aberdeenshire today – much of the past is still here to be seen and experienced.

8200–500 BC

EARLIEST TIMES

ABERDEEN AND ITS hinterland have been inhabited for at least 10,000 years. Recent excavations at Crathes, west of Aberdeen, revealed remains of what is believed to be the world's earliest calendar, created over several hundred years, starting in 8200 BC.

The first people who settled the area lived on the banks of the Rivers Dee and Don, which flow into the North Sea at Aberdeen. The area was covered by dense forest and so rivers and riverbanks were important for travel, the prehistoric equivalent of our roads and railways today. These early Mesolithic settlers would have used them to travel across the area with the seasons in their hunt for food. They ate what the land and water provided: ripe plants, berries and shellfish and they hunted wild animals and fish with their primitive weapons of flint and wood. Archaeologists have found pieces of flint and charcoal from this period near the River Dee at Crathes as well as traces of holes for wooden posts. These show that the Mesolithic people cleared areas of forest where they built settlements of small round huts.

Over the next 2,000 years farming gradually developed and spread across Europe. The new settlers who arrived on the banks of the Dee and Don about 6,000 years ago brought seeds to plant wheat and barley crops, as well as domestic animals.

These Neolithic, or New Stone Age, people also brought more advanced building techniques. In the 1970s, aerial photographs showed outlines in a field at Balbridie on the south bank of the Dee between Aberdeen and Crathes. Excavations provided exciting results – the foundations of a huge timber building more than 24 metres long and 13 metres wide, which would have had a roof 8.5 metres high. Inside, it had been divided by partitions providing communal living space for a family group and a grain storage barn, where thousands of grains of emmer wheat and barley were found. Though the first of its type to be excavated in Britain, the foundations were similar to those found previously in Central Europe and provided the first clue to the origins of these early farmers.

These New Stone Age people also left their mark around Aberdeen in the form of burial monuments. They lived in extended family groups and their dead were buried together in large communal chambers or tombs, which

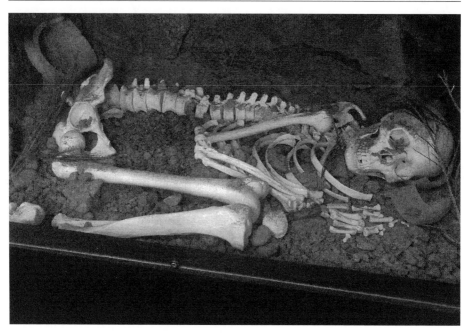

Full-scale reconstruction of a Burial Kist by Dr Sue MacLaughlin-Black. (Photo taken with kind permission of the Grassic Gibbon Centre, Arbuthnott)

were used for long periods before finally being sealed. Some were rectangular or wedge-shaped and sealed with earth and turf, which was scraped up rather than dug up, and are called Long Barrows today. Others, known as Long Cairns, were sealed by covering them with piles of boulders to form a cairn, although some are now overgrown with turf. Some were built on hilltops, easily seen from the surrounding countryside or from the sea. Others were built on lower-lying terraces by the rivers. All are huge – up to 80 metres long, 28 metres wide and 2.5 metres high. Over a period of about 2,000 years, some were altered and extended. Long Barrows and Long Cairns can still be seen in many locations in and around Aberdeen.

Towards the end of this period, about 4,500–5,000 years ago, ritual ceremonies were held in circular meeting places called Henges. These were level areas encircled by ditches with an outer bank of earth and were reached by a single, easily defended access or causeway through the bank and over the ditch. Today, we can only guess at the nature and meaning of the rituals held within these Henges.

The Beaker People, given that name because of their beaker-style pottery, came to north east Scotland about 4,500 years ago from what is now the Netherlands. Their dead were buried in individual graves with the corpse laid on its side with its legs drawn up. The grave was therefore quite small, only about 1 metre long. These are called Short Cists or Kists and were sometimes covered by a round cairn of stones – several of these can still be seen today in and around Aberdeen. Some Short Cists contain urns with cremated human remains. Also buried with these bodies were their distinctive pottery beakers and sometimes copper and bronze tools. However, it was the descendants of the Beaker People who really developed metal working skills, first in bronze and later in iron. This made tools and weapons much more efficient and gave rise to the Bronze and Iron Ages.

Around 4,000 years ago, the early Bronze Age people were responsible for constructing a large number of stone circles in north east Scotland. About a tenth of all the stone circles in Britain today are to be found in this area. Although those found here are relatively small, around 15 to 20 metres across, building them would have taken a huge amount of time and manpower.

Below *Easter Aquhorthies Stone Circle, near Inverurie. (Author's collection)*

Right *Recumbent stone and flankers. (© Crown Copyright reproduced courtesy of Historic Scotland www.historicscotlandimages.gov.uk)*

Stones were quarried and shaped with stone tools and moving each stone, even over flat ground, would have needed rollers underneath and two men for each tonne the stone weighed – some were around 24 tonnes! As most of these circles were set on high ground, many men would have been needed to manoeuvre the stones uphill and into position. Some would push, while others would move the rollers from the back to the front, so that the

WERE THE STONE CIRCLES PLACES OF SACRIFICE?

Why were these circles built? Were they used for rituals relating to death, ancestor worship or rites linked to the sun and the moon? Even within recent living memory, many people believed they were places of sacrifice where animals and perhaps even virgins were killed as an offering! It is certainly easy to imagine this when looking at the huge, altar-like recumbent slabs. However, today all have a peaceful unthreatening atmosphere and, as the sun and moon rise behind the recumbent at particular times of year, probably they were no more than a primitive form of calendar.

forward and upward momentum could be maintained.

Stone circles found in and around Aberdeen are different from those elsewhere in Britain, for they have a flat-topped 'recumbent' stone, usually on the south west side. The upright stones were set in a circle, sometimes a flattened circle, and graded by height, with the tallest two on either side of a huge block laid on its side – the recumbent stone. Many circles were built around earlier burial sites, with small burial cairns and cremated remains at their centre.

Around 2,500 years ago, metalworking skills developed from bronze to iron, giving the name to this period – the Iron Age. Settlements were built behind defences for the first time, possibly because of the influx of people fleeing from the invading Romans. These defences were usually timber fences called palisades, banks and ditches or stone walls. Natural defensive features were also used and many settlements were built on hilltops or coastal promontories. Some, called Crannogs, were built on manmade islands in lochs. Ironworking skills also allowed the development of more effective weapons, including swords for slashing enemies from a high vantage point, such as the top of a wall or perhaps even from horseback.

THE PICTS AND THE COMING OF THE ROMANS

ROUND 2,000 YEARS ago, the descendants of the Bronze and Iron Age peoples found themselves fighting to defend all they owned and all they knew. Their new enemies were the formidable Romans, with their highly trained, disciplined and battle-hardened army. The mighty Roman Empire had expanded its power base north into England and was now attacking the land they called Caledonia, which we know today as Scotland, and the natives, the Picts.

As the Roman Army and fleet moved north of the River Tay they encountered real resistance from these local tribes fiercely defending their native lands. By the year AD 83/84, the tensions and skirmishes led to a full-blown battle. History does not record a definite site for the Battle of Mons Graupius, although many historians believe it took place on the northern slopes of Bennachie. To the north west of present-day Aberdeen, this distinctive hill has six summits and is close to the eastern Grampian Mountains.

The invading Roman Army, under Gnaeus Julius Agricola, met the native defenders, partly on the hill slopes and partly on the flat land to the north. Roman historian Tacitus, writing the propaganda of the day to exaggerate the achievements of the Roman Army, tells us that several native tribes had united against them. He wrote that 30,000 men, led by Calgacus 'the Swordsman', were drawn up to meet the invaders. Although the Caledonians vastly outnumbered the Romans, their long slashing swords and chariots were no match for the invaders' close-combat tactics, cavalry and battle experience. The highly disciplined Roman cavalry reduced the natives' final advance to chaos, with wild-eyed, riderless horses and stray chariots rushing across the battlefield. The result was a decisive victory for the Romans. Thousands of natives – some reports say as many as 10,000 – were left dead or dying on the hillside, at the mercy of carrion crows and the wolves, lynx, bears and foxes which roamed Bennachie at that time.

With its mountainous terrain, few resources and savage natives, northern Caledonia was not a worthwhile prize for the Romans. The Gask Ridge wall and line of forts was constructed, following the natural barrier of the southern Grampian Mountains. This failed to keep the natives away from the civilised Roman settlements and Emperor Antoninus Pius ordered that a defensive

Aberlemno Church Stone: battle scene including a crow attacking a dead warrior (bottom right). (© Crown Copyright reproduced courtesy of Historic Scotland www.historicscotlandimages. gov.uk)

wall be built farther south. Known as the Antonine Wall, it formed the north west frontier of the Roman Empire. The Romans never settled among the Picts but may have ventured north of the wall occasionally, probably to retain control. Marching camps and roads were constructed, including some quite close to Aberdeen, which the Romans knew as Devana. At Peterculter, now part of the western outskirts of the city, are the remains of a marching camp called Normandykes. Excavations near Stonehaven in 2012–13 revealed part of the Gask Ridge Wall.

Perhaps it was the soldiers who patrolled the Antonine Wall who first gave a name to the painted warriors to the north. Roman writers described them as uncouth barbarians who lived in tents, wore neither clothes nor shoes, shared their women and brought up their children together. Perhaps this was more Roman propaganda, as we do know that these natives lived not in tents, but in large circular stone and timber huts. The Roman name *Picti*, the painted ones, foreshadows the name given much later to the same people by the original Scots, who called them *Cruithne*, the decorated ones. Around AD 500, these Scots moved from Northern Ireland with their king, Fergus Mor, and established the kingdom of Dalriada in what is now south west Scotland. We also know that the people we now call the Picts painted their faces and bodies with blue dye made from woad and were skilled artists and decorators. Much of what we know today about the Picts comes from the amazing carved standing stones they left behind.

We do not know why the Picts erected these stones. There are many in and near Aberdeen and some have been discovered within living memory. Perhaps they were boundary stones, marked the graves of important Pictish leaders, or had some ceremonial or ritual importance. They all have pictures or symbols carved on them, some also have intricate knotwork patterns and many had crosses added, often on the back of the stone, when the Picts embraced the Christian faith.

On the outskirts of modern Aberdeen, at St Fergus Church, Dyce, several Pictish stones can be seen today. The oldest is about 1,500 years old and carved with a stylised animal symbol, usually described as an elephant because

WHY THE MAIDEN STONE?

This stone is called the Maiden Stone because of a legend which tells the story of the daughter of the local landowner, the Laird of Balquhain. On her wedding day, she was baking in the kitchen when there was a knock at the door. She opened the door to find an extremely attractive young man standing there. They chatted for a while and he bet that he could build a road to the top of Bennachie before she could bake another batch of bannocks. If he succeeded, she was to become his bride. Believing she could not possibly lose, the girl agreed and set about her baking. As she put the bannocks in the oven, she looked out of the window and saw a road reaching to the very top of Bennachie. Instantly, she realised she'd been tricked by Auld Nick, the Devil himself. Terrified, she fled. But the Devil stretched out his long, long arm and touched her shoulder, turning her to stone and immortalising her forever as the Maiden Stone!

of its trunk-like nose. There are also very typical Pictish symbols on the stone, including a double disc and a Z-shaped rod, whose meaning we do not know. However, other stones have symbols which are much easier to understand, including primitive combs and mirrors. Some show men on horseback hunting stags with shaggy greyhound-like dogs, perhaps the forebears of the deerhound, the oldest of Scotland's dog breeds. Others are carved with battle scenes, including birds pecking the eyes of dead bodies, piles of headless bodies and severed heads.

One spectacular stone, known as the Maiden Stone, is not far from Aberdeen and close to Bennachie. It stands 3 metres high, is made of red granite and is around 1,200 years old. It features several weird Pictish beasts, a mirror and comb on one side while on the other are a large cross and a man between two fish-monsters, similar to creatures found on Roman altars. The narrow sides are carved with intricate knotwork. Although now eroded and indistinct in places, the different shapes can still be seen. The carving is remarkable, as granite is one of the hardest of all stones, and extremely difficult to smooth, far less carve, with only primitive tools.

The Maiden Stone, Pitcaple. (© Crown Copyright reproduced courtesy of Historic Scotland www.historicscotlandimages.gov.uk)

17

THE BLOODY SUCCESSION OF EARLY SCOTTISH KINGS

(including Macbeth)

MOST PEOPLE KNOW one story of Macbeth, as told by William Shakespeare in his famous tragic play. In this, Macbeth met three witches who foretold, among other things, that he would become King of Scotland. He fulfilled this prophesy by stabbing the elderly King Duncan to death in his bed. Assured that 'no man born of woman' could kill him, Macbeth believed he was almost immortal and continued to murder others, including the family of Macduff. Unknown to Macbeth, Macduff had been born by Caesarean, so was not 'born of woman'; it was he who finally killed Macbeth to avenge the murders of his own family.

The facts, so far as they are known, point to a very different story. In Moray, where Macbeth was Mormaer, or Earl, is Pitgaveny where he fought for his right to be King of Scotland. Here he killed King Duncan I in battle. About midway between the Moray blasted heath, where Shakespeare had Macbeth meet the three witches, and Glamis Castle, where much of the play is set, lies the village of Lumphanan. It was here, some miles west of Aberdeen, that Macbeth met his death in battle in 1057 at the hand of Malcolm Canmore, later King Malcolm III.

For around 500 years, since establishing their Kingdom of Dalriada in the west of what is now Scotland, the Scots had gradually expanded their territory by invading and exploiting the lands of the Picts. By the mid-800s the Picts, already weakened by Viking attacks, were finally defeated by the Scots, whose leader, Kenneth MacAlpin, became king of the Picts as well as the Scots, ruling over a fledgling kingdom they called Alba. The neighbouring lands to the south, Northumbria and Strathclyde, were ruled by sub-kings and straddled what is now the border with England.

Alba was a Celtic state where people spoke a slightly different form of the old language of the Picts, a Gaelic which the Scots had brought from Ireland together with their culture and harp music. The dominance of the Scots resulted in the name of the emerging country – Scotland – and a society which gave birth to the clan system. During their lifetime, reigning kings and chiefs would appoint their successors from their kinsmen, usually a brother, nephew or cousin who was fit, able and the right age to inherit the responsibility. Although it seems civilised, this system was open to abuse and led to intrigue and murder.

KENNETH II MURDERED BY AN EMBITTERED MOTHER

Following Kenneth MacAlpin's death in 859, ten kings each ruled Alba briefly. Then in 971 Kenneth II came to the throne and ruled for 24 years. Like the kings who preceded him, he found it hard to control the area south of Aberdeen called the Mearns, where one of the many to die by the king's sword was the son of the Mormaer of the Mearns and his wife Finella. At their Castle of Kincardine, near the foot of the mountain pass still called Cairn o' Mount, Finella plotted to avenge her son's death and had a special, elaborate tower constructed. Inside were rich tapestries which hid several loaded crossbows, all aimed at a statue of a king holding a golden apple. Feigning friendship and reconciliation, Finella invited King Kenneth to an opulent banquet. Afterwards, well-fed and probably somewhat inebriated, the king was taken by Finella to view the new tower where she enticed him to take the golden apple. Lifting the gift, King Kenneth unwittingly released multiple triggers and died in agony as crossbow bolts pierced his body from all angles.

Kenneth II had chosen his nephew, also Kenneth, as his successor. However, Kenneth II's son Malcolm had other ideas. He slew his cousin, seized the throne and became Malcolm II. The slaughter continued. Malcolm killed not only Kenneth III's son, but also all other members of his own family who might have a claim to the throne. Although Malcolm had no male heirs, his daughters had married influential leaders and he was determined to found a Royal House, his choice for king being his most favoured grandson Duncan. During his thirty-year reign, Malcolm killed every kinsman who might challenge Duncan for the throne, except Duncan's cousins Macbeth, son of the Mormaer of Moray, and Thorfinn the Mighty, son of the Earl of Orkney.

King Duncan was not the old man of Shakespeare's play and in fact came to the throne in his early thirties. Only six years later, as Duncan tried to take control of the north of Scotland, his cousin Macbeth, now Earl of Moray in his own right, defended his territory and challenged Duncan. The battle was fought at Pitgaveny near the River Lossie, northeast of Elgin. It was here that Duncan died at Macbeth's hand. Macbeth succeeded as king not by cold-blooded murder as told by Shakespeare, but in battle.

Macbeth reigned wisely for seventeen years. His wife, Gruoch, was far from being Shakespeare's Lady Macbeth character and became the first recorded Queen of Scotland. Although he and Gruoch had no children together, he appointed his stepson Lulach to succeed him. In 1050, the king was confident enough to leave Scotland to travel on pilgrimage to Rome with his cousin Thorfinn, and is reported to have scattered money there 'like seed' among the poor.

Duncan's son, Malcolm, was only nine when Macbeth slew his father, and was sent for safety to the English Court of King Edward the Confessor. There he grew up under English influence, but clearly felt he had a right to the throne of Scotland. Earl Siward the Strong of Northumbria supported Malcolm's claim and in 1054 marched north, defeating Macbeth's army at Dunsinane near Dunkeld, leaving the way clear for Malcolm to follow.

Known as Malcolm Canmore, meaning large head, Duncan's son at last headed to Scotland to avenge his father's death. Macbeth's men withdrew through the Cairn o' Mount pass over the eastern Grampian mountains, perhaps trying to reach Moray where Macbeth would expect more support from his own people. But Macbeth and his men were never to see Moray again. Although they reached the River Dee and crossed it, probably at the ford at Kincardine o' Neil, Malcolm's army was close behind and caught up with them nearby at Lumphanan Moss.

The tactics of the time were for the leader to order his men to dismount to meet the enemy. Macbeth probably took his place in the line with his best men, bidding them to hold their wooden shields firm against the weapons of Malcolm's men and to look for opportunities to attack. But warfare at this time was primitive, the victors being those who could hold their nerve through the shock of attack and violent contact.

There is no written record of the Battle of Lumphanan of 1057. However, local tradition points to Macbeth's Well, where the king is said to have quenched his

The view towards Lumphanan today from Cairn o' Mount. In Macbeth's time, the countryside would have been hidden by forest. (Author's collection)

thirst before the battle and to Macbeth's Stone, on which Malcolm is believed to have beheaded Macbeth. Legend has it that Macbeth's body was carried up the slope of Perkhill for temporary burial within an ancient cairn of stones, now called Macbeth's Cairn. Later, Macbeth's body was removed and taken to the holy island of Iona, traditional burial place of Scotland's early kings.

Although Lulach succeeded his stepfather as king, he reigned for only a few months before he and his supporters were slain by Malcolm, eager to take the throne for himself. As Malcolm III, he ruled for thirty-five years and attacked England persistently throughout his reign, dying in battle in 1093 while attacking Alnwick Castle. It seems his early upbringing at the English Court had little influence over his ambitions to extend his kingdom.

Macbeth's Well near Lumphanan.
(Author's collection)

HIDE YOUR WOMEN

The Norsemen are Coming!

THEY CAME TO plunder and rob and to take the women. Crossing the North Sea in their longships, relying on the east wind to fill their sails, the men rowed steadily whenever the wind dropped. They were warlike, these coastal dwellers, known as Vikings after the viks or inlets where they lived in Norway and Denmark. For around 400 years, few parts of Britain escaped their attention.

They also came to live in the lands they discovered and to trade with the natives. Many settled in Shetland, Orkney, the Hebrides and on the west coast of Scotland, from where they set out to explore and attack other parts. They left their settlements in the Northern Isles – Hjaltland and Hrossey, today's Shetland and Orkney. They sailed south to Katones, Caithness, and Sudrland, now Sutherland, and across the Moray Firth to Banffshire, Buchan and the North Sea coast of Aberdeenshire and Apardion, the name they gave to Aberdeen itself. They came to trade with the canny Aberdeen merchants and to settle fertile areas where the fishing was also good. But they did not always come in peace.

From around 950, Vikings harried the east coast, coming from the north and also from settlements to the south. Eric Bloodaxe, said to have become King of Norway after murdering all but one of his brothers, became King of Northumbria and lived in a palace in York. His wife was daughter of the King of Denmark and was believed to be a witch. Their sons, including perhaps the infamous Harald Greycloak, were among those who came to plunder Scotland's east coast. Here, they were defeated by natives, most likely on a hill near a place now called Cruden Bay, north of Aberdeen. This was obviously an attractive place, as Vikings later settled near this sandy bay, with its little river providing fresh water.

The Vikings harried the east coast, coming from their settlements in Caithness, Sutherland and Northumbria. (Myths of the Norsemen from the Eddas and Sagas)

KILLED BY A DEAD MAN!

Towards the end of the 800s, during the reign of Scottish King Donald II, the warlike Danes seized Northumbria, effectively cutting off contact between the Scots and the south. Around the same period, Sigurd the Mighty took control of the north of Scotland and even succeeded in taking the previously impregnable fortress of Dunnottar, set high on the cliffs south of Aberdeen. Sigurd revelled in this victory and cut off the Scots' leader's head, which he then hung from his saddle. But the Scot, Mael Brigte, known as The Bucked Tooth, fought back from the dead. As his head banged against the horse's flank, one of his filthy protruding teeth punctured Sigurd's leg – the mighty Sigurd went on to die an agonising death from blood poisoning.

Dunnottar Castle today – very different from the simple fortress of Viking times. (Author's collection)

By 1012, the Danes had settled near the sandy bay by the estuary of what is now called the Water of Cruden, where they built a fort on Hacklaw, the hill nearest the beach. Fearing the settlement needed reinforcing, Danish King Sweyn Haraldson sent his teenage son Cnut, or Canute, on the hazardous journey across the sea in charge of a large army. Already battle-hardened, the seventeen-year-old Canute had orders to defeat the Scots once and for all as

THE NORSEMEN'S SKULLS GRINNING HORRID

Another Danish raiding party was defeated when they came ashore from the Moray Firth in 1004, looting supplies for their storm-bound ships. What became known as the Battle of the Bloody Pits is thought to have been fought at present-day Bloodymire Farm, Longmanhill. Legend has it that the natives fought hard and fought dirty, with even the women involved, having filled their stockings with sand and stones to use as coshes! The blood-dripping, severed heads of at least three Danes were taken to St John's Church, near Gamrie, where the skulls remained displayed in the wall for centuries. In the 1830s, a visitor wrote, 'I have seen the Norsemen's skulls grinning horrid and hollow in the wall where they had been fixed directly east of the pulpit'.

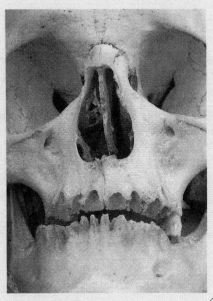

The Vikings' skulls 'grinning horrid'.
(Author's collection)

Sweyn, also known as Sueno, was keen to avenge the repeated losses he had suffered in earlier battles.

Tradition has it that King Malcolm II of Scotland preferred to harass the Danes by intercepting their food supplies with short, sharp attacks – what we might now call guerrilla tactics. He had fought and killed his kinsmen to become king, so he certainly had an appetite for battle and bloodshed. His reluctance to enter into full conflict with the Danes may be explained by the extremely difficult and bloody battle he had fought and won against them only two years before, at Mortlach in the hills to the west, where he lost three trusted leaders. Canute was determined, however, and indeed Malcolm's followers were spoiling for a real confrontation to see off the invaders. King Malcolm brought his troops to the flat land below Hacklaw, close to the sea. Here the battle was joined and vicious fighting raged all day, spreading inland along the river valley. Remains of the dead and their weapons have been found as far as 4 miles inland, although it was by the bay that most of the officers and nobility were slain.

As night fell, the survivors of both armies withdrew to lick their wounds. The sight which greeted them as dawn broke was so dreadful, with bodies strewn everywhere, that their thoughts turned to peace. This was the last major battle between the Scots and the Danes, with a treaty forged which was founded on the Christian faith and respected by both sides. The treaty decreed that the battlefield would become consecrated ground with the dead of both sides given an honourable Christian burial. King Malcolm ordered a chapel to be built on the site, which was dedicated to St Olaf, patron saint of Norway and Denmark. Under the terms of the treaty, the Danes and Norwegians withdrew from Scotland, with both sides agreeing to fight no more during the lifetime of Sweyn and Malcolm.

Canute lived to fight another day, and later in life became King of Denmark and England. Today, the consecrated ground is long forgotten and Cruden Bay's famous golf links lie on the site of the battleground and original chapel. The picturesque parish church, however, still bears the name of St Olaf and the battle lives on, over a thousand years later, in the name 'Croju Dane' or 'Crudane', which means death or slaughter of the Danes.

Many Viking warriors were skilful archers.
(Heimskringla, *drawn by Christian Krohg*)

Much of the Vikings' contact with the town of Aberdeen, Apardion, was in trading with local merchants. However, in the early 1100s, Eystein, an illegitimate son of Norwegian King Magnus Barefoot, became joint King of Norway with his brothers Sigurd and Olaf. Olaf died young and while Sigurd was away fighting the Crusades in Moorish Spain and the Holy Land, Eystein served Norway well, venturing west across the North Sea. In Caithness, he captured Earl (or Jarl) Harald Maddadson, succeeding against the Jarl's large thirty-bench galley and eighty men with only three small cutters. Once the Jarl's ransom of three marks of gold was paid, Eystein sailed south to the market town of Apardion, where he robbed the town and slew many men, breaking their swords. This was all recorded later the same century in *Geisli* by Icelandic poet Einar Skúlason:

In Apardion there fell
All the folk, as I have heard;
The swords were broken
Yonder the king plundered.

THE WARS OF INDEPENDENCE

'Braveheart' v. 'The Hammer of the Scots'

RELATIONS BETWEEN SCOTLAND and England had been peaceful for some time when Edward 'Longshanks' became King Edward I of England in 1272. King Alexander III of Scotland had inherited the crown from his father in 1249 at the age of eight, for now it was accepted that the throne passed from father to eldest son, or if necessary to a younger son or a daughter. Two years after becoming king, Alexander married the young daughter of Henry III of England, Margaret, with whom he had two sons and a daughter.

Scotland's history may well have been very different had any of these children survived, but Queen Margaret and all three children died within a few years of each other. However, their daughter, married to Erik II of Norway, died giving birth to a daughter who survived. This child, also Margaret and known as 'The Maid of Norway', was Alexander's sole heir and only three years old when, in 1286, Alexander was thrown from his horse and killed.

Margaret never saw Scotland, for she died in 1290 on board the ship carrying her from Norway to her kingdom and her agreed marriage to Edward I's young son, Edward. For two years afterwards,

Scotland was without a king, queen or ruler. The main contenders to be king were John Balliol and Robert Bruce, both descendants of David I. Edward I was asked to decide who should be king. He was already using the title 'Overlord of the land of Scotland' and the price he demanded for his mediation was high – all possible successors to Margaret must recognise the King of England as their feudal superior.

Edward's choice was John Balliol, who was proclaimed king in 1292 on the symbolic Stone of Scone and paid homage to Edward just a few weeks later. Edward's demands increased until eventually Balliol rebelled. Rather than providing the military support against France that Edward demanded, in 1295 Balliol made a treaty with the King of France. This became known as The Auld Alliance and was an important pact for centuries between the two nations against their common enemy, England.

Edward now had the excuse he wanted. He marched his battled-hardened, professional soldiers north to meet Balliol's inexperienced and poorly armed men. The English swept into Scotland, sacking Berwick, massacring its inhabitants then routing Balliol's apology for an army at Dunbar. Many castles fell to the English and in 1296, with even Edinburgh Castle in English hands, Balliol surrendered. Near Brechin in Angus, south of Aberdeen, he was stripped of his royal insignia and taken south while Edward continued his rampage through Scotland. His ruthlesness resulted in his becoming known as 'The Hammer of the Scots'. One of Edward's spoils of war was the historic Stone of Scone, or Stone of Destiny, on which all Scottish kings had been proclaimed. Edward removed the Stone and took it to Westminster Abbey.

In 1296, Edward and his army camped in a field close to Kincardine o'Neil, not far from the battlefield where Macbeth had been killed around 250 years earlier. It is said that there were few men left in Kincardine o'Neil to protect their women and children. When the English arrived they sacked the village, stealing all the food and raping the women before leaving them and their children to starve.

These scenes were replayed across Scotland. At Lanark in the west, the English killed many, including the brother and wife of a man called William Wallace. Enraged by their actions, he took his revenge by killing the English sheriff of Lanark, and so started the legend on which the film *Braveheart* was based.

In fact, little is known of Wallace's early life and many stories about him were originally written by a poet called Blind Harry, who lived 200 years later and could not possibly have experienced the events he claimed to have witnessed. They were, however, great stories and when Blind Harry's poem about Wallace was eventually printed around 1508, it outsold every other printed book in Scotland with the exception of the Bible.

Statue of William Wallace, Union Terrace, Aberdeen. (Author's collection)

Wallace is known to have belonged to a landowning family, but was not a nobleman. He was well travelled and almost certainly had fought in battle. His great ally was Andrew de Moray, from the same part of north east Scotland as Macbeth, and it is possible that many of the exploits 'reported' by Blind Harry may have been carried out by de Moray, rather than Wallace. The two succeeded in drawing together an effective and disciplined army which included not only knights and nobles, but also landowners and more lowly Scots. Using clever tactics they decimated the English Army at the Battle of Stirling Bridge, killing and skinning the English Treasurer Cressingham, whose flayed skin was cut up and distributed among the victorious Scots. Legend has it that Wallace made a belt for his sword with his piece of Cressingham skin. Andrew de Moray died from wounds he received at the Battle of Stirling Bridge – perhaps

Wallace is said to have accessed the castle by Fiddlehead Rock; today, visitors use a path. (Author's collection)

his early death is the reason his name is rarely remembered alongside Wallace's.

Historical records show Blind Harry's poem to be inaccurate. At the time when Dunnottar and Aberdeen were burned, Wallace was actually carrying out raids in Central Scotland. However, in 1298, vastly outnumbered by Edward's army, his men were finally defeated at the Battle of Falkirk. Resigning his Guardianship of Scotland, Wallace fled to France.

On his return to Scotland in 1305, Wallace was hunted down and finally betrayed by a fellow Scot. Accused of treason by a king he never acknowledged, he was taken to stand trial in London. His sentence was barbaric: he was hanged, drawn and quartered – after the hanging, while still alive, he was castrated, his bowels torn out, then he was beheaded and his body cut into quarters. His head was displayed on a pike above London Bridge, and the four parts of his body were sent to cities including Newcastle, Perth and Berwick. Most reports state the fourth city was Stirling but some claim it was Aberdeen, where it is said an arm and half his torso were displayed near St Machar's Cathedral. This would serve to warn others of the punishment for any tempted to follow in Wallace's footsteps.

DEATH BY FIRE OR DEATH BY DROWNING!

According to Blind Harry, Wallace brought his men to Dunnottar, the clifftop castle on a headland some miles south of Aberdeen. This castle had huge strategic importance; it controlled the main north–south route along the coast and was in English hands. Wallace was determined to take it. His men were untrained but their reputation preceded them – apparently the well-drilled English soldiers were terrified and took refuge in the chapel, the only stone building on the headland at that time. If they believed the Scots would respect the religious sanctuary, they were wrong. Wallace and his men crept over the cliffs of Fiddlehead Rock, onto the headland and into the castle. Discovering the English soldiers in the chapel, Wallace ordered it to be burned, condemning them to a horrific death, with burning roof timbers falling among them. Those who escaped the fire leapt to their deaths in the sea.

Blind Harry recounts that Wallace then continued to Aberdeen, where the English set fire to the town and retreated into Aberdeen Castle. Having tried but failed to take it, Wallace ordered the Scots to set fire to the 100 English ships anchored nearby in the River Dee estuary and to slaughter all the English they could find. According to historian John of Fordun, all citizens showing any English sympathies were put to death, although Wallace did spare the lives of women, children and priests.

THE WARS OF INDEPENDENCE

King Robert the Bruce

ROBERT BRUCE, GRANDSON of Balliol's rival for the throne, is better known to Scots as Robert The Bruce. He was initially torn between loyalty to Scotland and loyalty to Edward I. In 1297 he declared support for Wallace but the following year fought for the English at the Battle of Falkirk – over the years he changed allegiance five times. However, finally he realised he was the natural leader his country so desperately needed and made a pact with the Bishop of St Andrews to strengthen his claim to the throne. The Comyn family, who dominated Buchan, the area north of Aberdeen, was bitterly opposed to Bruce. 'The Red Comyn', one of the most powerful men in Scotland, was Bruce's main rival for the throne. Early in 1306 they agreed to meet in Greyfriars Church, Dumfries, and left their swords outside the door. They argued, Bruce drew his dagger and stabbed Comyn to death in front of the altar. This sacrilegious murder left the way clear for Bruce to be proclaimed King of Scotland at Scone, despite the absence of the Stone of Destiny.

We know a great deal about Bruce's exploits from the poem *The Brus*, written by Archdeacon of St Machar's Cathedral, Aberdeen, John Barbour, whose life overlapped Bruce's. His writing used contemporary information and possibly even eyewitness accounts. Barbour tells us that from Scone, Bruce and his men travelled the country, raising support wherever they went. In June 1306, following a crushing defeat, Bruce and his men took to the hills, living rough before taking refuge in Aberdeen. The respite was brief as the English soon learned where he was and so the king, his men and his family headed into rural Aberdeenshire. For their own safety, his queen, Elizabeth de Burgh, and nine-year-old daughter Marjory were sent to join his sisters at

Bruce's coronation at Scone; memorial, Hazlehead Park, Aberdeen. (Author's collection)

Kildrummy Castle, in the care of his brother Neil and the Earl of Atholl.

Kildrummy Castle in Aberdeenshire commanded an important strategic position at the point where the main routes from south, north and north east converged, and it had been taken and occupied twice by Edward I. Although in 1306 this seemed a place of safety for Bruce's family, the Earl of Atholl soon discovered that English troops were approaching and decided to take the king's family farther north. Edward, Prince of Wales and his troops besieged the castle which Neil Bruce struggled valiantly to defend. It is said, and partly confirmed by Barbour, that the English bribed Osbourne, the local blacksmith, promising him all the gold he could carry if he could help break the siege. This he did by setting fire to the castle's Great Hall, in use as a temporary grain store. Neil Bruce was captured and taken south to be hanged, drawn and quartered, while Osbourne became a victim of English treachery – they did pay him, but melted the gold and poured it down his throat, killing him. At Tain in the north, the queen, princess and Bruce's sisters were captured by the Earl of Ross, a supporter of Bruce's rivals, the Comyns. They were handed over to Edward I and imprisoned in England. The Earl of Atholl was executed and Kildrummy Castle was partly demolished.

Following his defeats and with his family held captive, Bruce was despondent; this was the time of the famous spider story, which some say happened in a cave near Oldmeldrum, north west of Aberdeen. The legend tells that, lying low in a cave, Bruce was inspired by the determination of a spider

Bruce believed his family would be safe at Kildrummy Castle; this is how it looks today. (© Crown Copyright reproduced courtesy of Historic Scotland www.historicscotlandimages. gov.uk)

to make a cobweb, trying repeatedly until it succeeded. Following the spider's example, Bruce decided to try again and in 1308 he finally defeated his enemy, the Comyn Earl of Buchan, at the Battle of Barra near Oldmeldrum. Bruce's brother Edward pressed home the advantage, following the Comyns into Buchan and virtually exterminating the family and their supporters, putting all to the sword and burning farms, crops, livestock and forests in an action called the Harrying of Buchan. At that time Bruce had been quite ill and had even been carried on a litter during the campaign. He spent the winter in Aberdeen recovering his strength.

In 1314, Bruce defeated the English army at Bannockburn, winning independence for Scotland. Following this historic victory, in gratitude for the assistance of its citizens, King Robert the Bruce rewarded Aberdeen with a gift of the Royal Stocket Forest, land still known today as 'The Freedom Lands'. In fact, although the king initially granted Aberdeen custodianship of the Forest,

BRUCE AND ABERDEEN CASTLE

Aberdonians often tell stories from this period, although there are no records in the city archives or *The Brus* to support them.

One tells how, some time after Bruce's victory at the Battle of Barra, the citizens of Aberdeen rose up and, using the words 'Bon Accord' as a rallying cry or password, stormed the castle. They seized it from the English in Bruce's name and ruthlessly put every last English soldier to the sword. This story was already accepted by the 1670s, when Aberdeen's coat of arms with the motto 'Bon Accord' was approved with the explanation: 'The word Bon-Accord was given them by King Robert Bruce, for killing all the English in the night, in their town, the word being that night 'Bon-Accord.'

Is this myth or fact? It is recorded that the castle was still held by the English in the summer of 1308, when it was besieged by land and sea by Bruce's troops, and that it ceased to exist after that year. Perhaps it was taken and flattened by Bruce's men – they might even have been assisted by local citizens shouting 'Bon Accord!'

this was hardly an outright gift as from 1319 an annual payment of £213 6s 8d was required for the right to develop the area. The king also granted Charters, giving the burgesses and community of Aberdeen the ownership of the burgh itself, allowing Aberdeen to retain much of the dues or taxes collected from its citizens that had previously been paid to the Royal Treasury. This, together with the right to develop the Stocket Forest, allowed Aberdeen to prosper. The king also ensured that funds were made available to complete the first bridge over the River Don at Aberdeen. Called the Brig of Balgownie, this gave safe access to and from the coast to the north and the fertile lands of Buchan. This bridge is still in use today, although not open to motor traffic.

The John Barbour memorial shows Bruce addressing his troops at Bannockburn, The Brig o' Balgownie and Barbour writing his epic poem The Brus. *Carved by Roland Fraser, it is in the Cathedral Church of St Machar, Old Aberdeen. (Photo taken with kind permission of Cathedral Church of St Machar)*

THE BLOODY BATTLE
OF HARLAW

NOT ALL DISAGREEMENTS were between the Scots and the English. One of the bloodiest battles was fought in 1411 at Harlaw, north west of Aberdeen. Here, local nobles, lairds (landowners), the Provost of Aberdeen and many of the town's most important citizens joined the Earl of Mar to defend the area against an aggressive invasion by Donald, Lord of the Isles. So much blood was spilled that rivers ran red and the battle became known as Reid (or Red) Harlaw.

Until Alexander III finally defeated the Vikings at the Battle of Largs in 1263, the north west of Scotland had effectively been a separate kingdom. By the early 1400s, although nominally part of Scotland, the Hebrides and the area known today as Argyll were ruled by the Lord of the Isles, Donald MacDonald. An Oxford-educated nobleman of both Norse and Gaelic descent, Donald married the sister of the Earl of Ross and aimed to expand his kingdom to include the Earldom of Ross and Skye. This was a vast area which included lands in Aberdeenshire, at that time under the charge of the Earl of Mar.

The rest of Scotland had been ruled somewhat ineffectively by the first of the Stewart kings, Robert II, who made no attempt to control either the MacDonalds in the north west or the Douglases in the Borders. Ultimately his eldest son became Guardian of the Realm, or Regent, although a disabling kick from a horse resulted in this son being ruled unfit to govern even before he took the throne as Robert III. This left the way clear for his ambitious and ruthless brother the Earl of Fife, later Duke of Albany, to become Regent – king in all but name. Another brother was Alexander, Earl of Buchan, the notorious 'Wolf of Badenoch', remembered today for having burned Elgin Cathedral.

Ineffectual rule continued and lawlessness escalated. The gap widened between the civilised and prosperous Lowlands and the Highlands, perceived as barbaric by Lowlanders. The Regent's nephew, Alexander, illegitimate son of the Wolf of Badenoch, took the title of Earl of Mar in 1404. This he did by seizing and killing the existing Earl and besieging his castle at Kildrummy, threatening to burn it down if his widow refused to marry him – the countess had no choice but to agree. Four years later she, too, was dead and Albany was implicated in two suspicious

Coats of Arms, Harlaw Monument: (left to right) *MacLean of Duart; Donald, Lord of the Isles; Earl of Mar. (Author's collection)*

deaths. Robert III's eldest son, David, was imprisoned and starved to death on Albany's orders; the king sent his surviving son, James, to France for safety. But he was captured by pirates and handed over to Henry IV of England, who imprisoned the young prince in the Tower of London.

The Earl of Ross, Alexander Leslie, also died in suspicious circumstances at Albany's castle in Falkland. Donald, Lord of the Isles claimed the Earldom of Ross and Skye on behalf of his wife, the sister of the late Earl. Albany claimed it on behalf of his infant granddaughter, the late Earl's daughter, whom he made his Ward, and declared himself Lord of the Ward of Ross. Donald and his kinsmen, a force said to be 6,000 strong, marched through Ross to Inverness where they burned the bridge and the castle. Other Highland clans joined them, including the MacLeods, MacLeans, MacIntoshes and Camerons.

The Earl of Mar and his friends, Sir Alexander Forbes, Sir Alexander Irvine of Drum, Sir Alexander Keith of Grandholme and Sir John Menzies of Pitfodels were frequent visitors to a tavern near Aberdeen Harbour, kept by Robert Davidson, Provost of Aberdeen. The Earl was therefore able to call on their support when he realised his own land and claim to the Earldom of Ross were threatened by the Lord of the Isles. He called them to a meeting at Kildrummy Castle, where they were joined by Sir Alexander Ogilvy, the

Coats of Arms, Harlaw Monument: (left to right) *Irvine of Drum; Aberdeen; Provost Davidson. (Author's collection)*

33

THE LEGEND OF HOSIE

One young local man by the name of Hosie was due to be married on 24 July 1411. Instead, he found himself fighting for his life against the wild caterans and, following the battle, was captured by them and taken to the Isles. Some time later, he escaped and returned to Harlaw, only to find his beloved married to another man. It is said he climbed the slopes of Bennachie, where he and his love had so often met, and there he lay down and died of a broken heart. He was buried where he lay and later a spring bubbled up nearby – a spring which is said to flow not with water but with Hosie's tears!

Sheriff of Angus; Sir James Scrymgeour, the Constable of Dundee; and other landowners – Frasers, Gordons, Leslies and Skenes. Rumours of the band of approaching Highlanders, their number now around 10,000, spread to Aberdeen, resulting in support from a large number of influential and important citizens.

It was reported that Donald intended to sack and plunder the royal town of Aberdeen and enforce his authority on the country as far as the River Tay. Donald's men were described as 'occupying the district in such large and savage numbers like locusts, all those ... who saw them were alarmed, and every man was afraid ... ' By July 1411 Donald and his Highlanders were camped less than 20 miles from Aberdeen, close to the farm or fermtoun of Harlaw, almost in the shadow of Bennachie. This was a good defensive position on a plateau close to the confluence of the River Urie and Lochter Burn and was bounded by both.

Many local men marched to Harlaw, under the leadership of Provost Robert Davidson, to join the Earl of Mar in the fight against the Highland caterans. They camped lower down the River Urie, on the spit of land where it joins the River Don, close to a motte and bailey castle, stronghold of the Earls of the Garioch.

On the morning of 24 July 1411, Mar and his supporters struck camp and crossed the Urie to reach the Highlanders' position. Mar split his men into two divisions, with Ogilvy and Scrimgeour leading the first attack and his own division assembling *schiltron*, close formations of spearsmen. The Gaelic Harlaw battle song tells that Donald's forces were in three divisions with Hector Roy Maclean of Duart, 'Red Hector of the Battles' at the head of his clan, leading the right wing in the place of honour. Chief of Clan MacIntosh, Callum Beg, led on the left, while Donald himself commanded the central force.

Donald's three divisions forced back Mar's attack and it is believed that Provost Davidson was killed during this initial push back. Each side fought hard in hand-to-hand combat. All fighting would have been on foot, although the nobles and lairds would have arrived on horseback. Only they would have worn armour of any sort, most likely plate armour for Mar's men and chain mail for the clan chiefs. The main fighting force

Harlaw Monument and Bennachie, near Inverurie. (Author's collection)

would have been totally unprotected – any sort of weighty armour would have slowed them down. Warfare was still primitive, with bravery and battle experience counting for much against novices, their nerve shattered by the shock of close combat. They fought with swords, axes, spears, lances and perhaps even their bare fists. Man fought man, among them Alexander Irvine, Laird of Drum, against Red Hector of the Battles, chief of the Macleans. After their very personal battle, both lay dead.

Donald lost 900 men that day, while Mar lost 600 – a larger proportion of his force. Both sides claimed victory. However, Donald retreated to the Hebrides, his claim to the Earldom of Ross unsuccessful. Mar's losses included a long list of nobles, lairds, citizens and the war-like Provost of Aberdeen. One history of the battle, based on contemporary writing, states: 'The whole plateau is red with blood; from the higher points to the lower blood flows in streams ... '

Today, a monument stands near to the site, commissioned by Aberdeen City Council on the 500th anniversary of the battle. Six panels were added for the 600th anniversary, with brightly painted shields of the main protagonists of both sides who fought and died on that blood-soaked plateau. These include not only Donald, Lord of the Isles and the Earl of Mar, but also the Provost of Aberdeen. In 2011, a simple cross was erected and unveiled in nearby Chapel of Garioch kirkyard as a memorial to all the Leslies who died in the battle.

PIRACY ON THE HIGH SEAS!

DONALD, LORD OF the Isles was a well-educated nobleman but his adversaries at Harlaw, the Earl of Mar and Provost Davidson, were acknowledged pirates! They were far from being Aberdeen's only pirates, but they used their exalted positions to protect themselves. Although brought to court, Provost Davidson was free to go about his business, with officialdom turning a blind eye to his activities. Other more lowly pirates were not so lucky.

Since people started using boats and ships to transport goods, pirates have made it their mission to attack and steal them. Around 3,000 years ago, the Sea People of the Eastern Mediterranean were the earliest recorded pirates, whereas the Vikings are perhaps the best-known and most successful. Today piracy continues to be a real threat to shipping, goods and life in some parts of the world. The capture of ships, their cargo, passengers and crew need not be confined to the high seas, however – acts of piracy could, and can, be committed on rivers, lakes and even in harbours.

From the 1100s onwards, Aberdeen was a Royal Burgh, entitled to trade with countries overseas. The natural anchorage in the Dee estuary had been

(Drawn by Oren neu dag)

in use as a harbour for some time before 1136, when the king gave permission for ships using the harbour to be taxed. As a seafaring and trading burgh, Aberdeen was affected by piracy for centuries. Its shipping suffered pirate attacks but at the same time the port was a place where pirated goods were sold and ships were rigged and equipped for piracy. Several of Aberdeen's citizens were themselves pirates.

In the 1300s, most of Aberdeen's legitimate trade was with other parts of Scotland and with England, but there was also brisk trading with Holland and the Hanseatic League ports, mainly Lübeck, Hamburg and Danzig, with less frequent sailings to France and occasionally Spain. Aberdeen's main exports were wool and salmon.

At that time navigation tools were primitive, usually comprising only a crude compass and perhaps a basic instrument such as an astrolabe or cross-staff to sight the Pole Star. The only guidance was *The Book of the Sea*, which gave silhouettes of headlands, depth soundings and directions based on these. As a result, vessels sailed within sight of land wherever possible. Merchant ships would sail in company or convoy for mutual protection. However, the risks were still great, with losses from natural causes, including storm, human error and plague, as well as piracy. Trading ships would normally be away from their home port for a year as, with only square-rigged sails, they were dependent on the seasonal changes of wind direction in the North Sea and the Baltic. It was therefore often many months before shipowners realised their vessels had been captured.

Privateering was a legitimised form of piracy, with the seizure of ships and goods carried out in the name of the government. In theory this only happened in wartime, against enemy merchant shipping, but in practice it was much more widespread. If the captain was in possession of a Letter of Marque and Reprisal, he could effectively commit legal piracy. Attacking and seizing a ship while not in possession of these Letters was treated as a serious crime, the penalty being death by hanging. Proof of ownership was another means of legitimising piracy and shipmasters would rush to the magistrate immediately on arrival in port with a 'new' ship to obtain a proof of ownership document.

In the mid-1300s, Aberdeen piracy was so prevalent that the burgh appointed a commissioner to deal with claims for compensation, particularly from Flanders. By the end of the century the Earl of Mar was the government's law enforcer for the north of Scotland and admiral for the North Sea. His legal

Ships in close combat. (Library of Congress Prints and Photographs Division, LC-USZ62-69337)

PIRATES HANGED AT ABERDEEN HARBOUR

In 1596, the Provost and council certainly did not look kindly upon four men who captured a ship, its cargo and crew from Burntisland in Fife. Forced ashore by storms in Cromarty, north of Inverness, they were eventually brought to Aberdeen to stand trial at the burgh's expense. This was considerable and included the cost of horses and escorts to transport the prisoners, legal payments, a total of £3 5s to build the gallows and pay the hangman – and £4 for the council officers' supper! Robert Brewster, Andrew Brown, John Jackson and Robert Laird were hanged on the specially built gallows near the Blockhouse at Pocra Quay. Without the right connections, and perhaps forced into piracy by economic hardship, they paid the ultimate price for a crime which their lords and masters blatantly committed with no redress.

advisor was Aberdeen Provost, wine merchant and tavern keeper Robert Davidson. More and more piracy was blamed on Scots at this time, with merchants from Gouda and Harlem in the Low Countries particularly vociferous in their complaints. No specific names were given although the Earl of Mar was implicated time and again. In 1409 two English ships, the *Marie*, owned by Lord Mayor of London Richard 'Dick' Whittington, and the *Thomas*, were captured by Scottish pirates. Robert Davidson was certainly involved in the seizure of the *Thomas*, whose cargo he sold in Amsterdam.

The Dutch and the Hanseatic League each imposed embargoes on Scottish trade, including wool from Aberdeen, and some League members took Davidson to court in Paris. However, the well-connected Davidson had been given a guarantee of Safe Conduct by the French Government which effectively stopped the court case. He even persuaded Aberdeen Burgh Council to send a letter to Danzig expressing its disbelief that the Provost was involved,

blaming the Dutch and demanding recompense for Davidson!

During the 1500s, particularly the second part of the century, there was intermittent hostility between Scotland and England and between England and France, resulting in the issue of many Letters of Marque and Reprisal, which were consistently abused. Piracy, masquerading as privateering, escalated to the point where it was the subject of letters from Elizabeth I to Mary, Queen of Scots complaining about the losses sustained by English and Welsh merchants as a result of Scottish piracy. These losses included 60 tuns of wine, equivalent to 69,000 litres! Pirate Robert Patterson from Dundee successfully sold wood, spars, barrels, ropes and anchors in Aberdeen from a Norwegian ship he had seized. The Provost of the time had at first ordered the ship to be arrested, but later released it on condition that Aberdeen's good name would not be sullied and the burgh gave Patterson a testimonial stating that none of the Norwegian crew had been harmed. Despite such attempts to keep its good name, by 1573 Aberdeen was known as a place where pirates could rig-out ships and sell stolen goods. That year the Privy Council of Scotland wrote to the burgh, ordering the Provost and magistrates to arrest a Dutch ship which had been seized by the notorious pirate Captain Halkerstoun and taken to Aberdeen. The council members were threatened with being exposed as pirates themselves and charged along with Halkerstoun and his crew if they failed to do this.

Aberdeen ships were sometimes the victims of piracy. One vessel, the *Lyon*, was returning to Aberdeen from France in 1673 with a cargo of paper, hats and hoops when it was attacked off the English coast by a Dutch ship and sailed to Holland. The cargo was sold and a merchant on board, William Logan, was held hostage for a ransom of £145. Hostage-taking and ransoms became more frequent during the 1600s and Aberdeen ships continued to be the target of pirates into the 1700s. However, gradually the focus of piracy was moving away from Europe, following the lucrative trading routes with the New World. This was the period when piracy, as we now understand it, really flourished in the Caribbean. Today, pirates target shipping in the Indian Ocean, particularly the waters off Somalia and the Gulf of Aden.

BURN OF BLOOD

Mary, Queen of Scots Clips
The Cock o' the North's Wings

MARY WAS JUST six days old when she became Queen of Scots on the death of her father, James V, in 1542. Nine months later she was crowned at Stirling Castle, where she lived with her mother, Mary of Guise. Aged six she was sent to France for her own safety and was raised there under the protection of her powerful Guise uncles, while her mother remained in Scotland and contrived to become Regent in 1554. Two years later, during a royal visit to Huntly Castle, the Regent Mary was warned that the Gordon family was becoming too powerful.

Over the centuries, the Gordons' support for the Stewart monarchs had ensured their place as the most powerful family in the north of Scotland. At Strathbogie, given to them by Robert the Bruce, they built a magnificent palace which they called Huntly Castle. The family's influence increased and the 4th Earl became known as 'The Cock o' the North'. It was he who hosted an extravagant royal visit by Mary of Guise in 1556. So lavish was his hospitality that after a few days, the Regent Mary suggested leaving to relieve the burden on him. In response, the Earl showed her the castle's vaults and larders, groaning with provisions, clear evidence of his conspicuous wealth. This prompted the French Ambassador to advise that action should be taken to curb the Gordons' position of power before they became a real threat to the Royal House of Stewart.

In France, the queen grew into an attractive, well-educated, musical and athletic woman who spoke several languages fluently and carried herself with grace and elegance. At the age of fifteen she married the Dauphin, who became King Francis II on the death of his father in 1559. The French proclaimed him King of France and Scotland, alienating the Scots, who saw this as the end of the Auld Alliance. The same year, a Protestant rising overthrew Mary of Guise as Regent and in 1560 Protestantism became the official religion of Scotland. When Queen Mary was suddenly widowed she returned to Scotland, arriving in Edinburgh in 1561. Despite being politically naïve, she was astute enough to understand she must be seen to support the Protestant government, although she herself was Catholic. She turned for advice to her illegitimate half-brother, James Stewart, who staunchly supported Protestant Reform.

The Cock o' the North's Huntly Castle as it is today. (© Crown Copyright reproduced courtesy of Historic Scotland www.historicscotland-images.gov.uk)

The Cock o'the North, the Earl of Huntly, was a Catholic and assumed Mary would support the Catholic cause. Before she left France, he sent a secret message proposing she should land at Aberdeen, where 20,000 men would await her arrival and restore her kingdom to the old religion. The queen's decision to ignore this invitation was both a clear signal she did not favour Catholics and also a personal slight to Huntly – the first of several insults. During the queen's absence, he had assumed the vacant titles of Earl of Mar and Earl of Moray, administering these estates which adjoined his own. His ambitions were thwarted when Queen Mary bestowed the Earldoms of Mar and Moray on her Protestant half-brother, James Stewart.

On the Earl of Moray's advice, the queen travelled north on a royal progress, arriving in Aberdeen in August 1562 with her Protestant lords and a guard of Lothian spearsmen. Welcomed by the Provost of Aberdeen, she stayed with Bishop Gordon, holding Court in his palace in Old Aberdeen. Huntly did not attend Court but sent his countess to deliver an invitation to visit their castle at Strathbogie. The queen chose not to although she passed within a few miles as she made her way to Inverness.

Huntly's third son, Sir John Gordon, had been imprisoned for injuring a rival, but had escaped twice and been given shelter by his father. Rumoured to be the queen's lover, Sir John was certainly infatuated with her, believing she was a helpless prisoner of the Protestants whom he must rescue. He and his associates shadowed the royal party through his family lands between Aberdeen and Inverness, but were held at a distance by the queen's bodyguards. Queen Mary was outraged and sent a summons to Huntly, requiring him to surrender the keys to his three castles. He sent the keys for Auchindoun and Findlater, but refused to give up his seat at Huntly or to appear before the Privy Council – his countess delivered this message. Huntly and Sir John Gordon were declared outlaws and an armed detachment was sent to bring them in. Huntly, however, was warned just in time and managed to escape through the back door of his castle.

Despite his recent boast that he could raise 20,000 supporters, Huntly now found his friends and allies in the area had little appetite for battle, particularly against the queen and the Royal Army. The main support he could muster was from his own family, even though some Gordons chose to join the queen's forces. By 28 October 1562, his entire force was at most 800 and possibly as few as 500 – a poor showing. They camped close to Aberdeen at Cullerlie, on what is still known as Gordon's Moss.

In the name of the queen, the Earl of Moray had raised reinforcements from Angus and the Mearns. He had 2,000 men including cavalry and trained soldiers armed with spears and long-barrelled guns called arquebuses. Following a skirmish with Moray's vanguard, the Gordons retreated onto the higher ground of the Hill o' Fare. So many in the vanguard were Huntly's former allies that he did not believe them to be real enemies, and it seems they fought only half-heartedly. Under Moray, the trained forces pressed home their attack. Gunfire from the arquebusiers drove Huntly from the hilltop down to the boggy ground where the Corrichie Burn rises. It is said the queen watched from near the summit, where an outcrop still bears the name the Queen's Chair. The Royal Cavalry attacked next, cornering the Gordons until the footsoldiers of the Lothian Pikemen could finish the task of annihilating them. Contemporary accounts report the Gordons were 'put upoun their bakkis with speiris

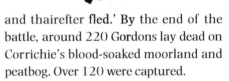

Cast of the effigy of Mary, Queen of Scots, commissioned by her son James VI and I for her tomb in Westminster Abbey. (Photo taken with kind permission of Blairs Museum Trust)

and thairefter fled.' By the end of the battle, around 220 Gordons lay dead on Corrichie's blood-soaked moorland and peatbog. Over 120 were captured.

The prisoners were tried and convicted, and five were hanged just two days after the battle. The queen granted Sir George Gordon, heir to the title, a stay of execution. Sir John Gordon was condemned to be beheaded. It is said the queen and her court watched from a window as his sentence was carried out in the Castlegate by an executioner 'so awkward that he wounded Sir John several times before severing his head'.

THE END OF THE COCK O' THE NORTH

Huntly himself surrendered his sword to Queen Mary's bodyguard. Placed on a horse, he was paraded before his captors, utterly humiliated. Suddenly and silently, without any blow being struck, he fell from his horse, 'stark dead'. It seems the corpulent earl had succumbed to apoplexy, which today would be called a stroke. Slung over two creels, his body was unceremoniously transported to Aberdeen and dumped on the pavement outside the Tolbooth in the Castlegate.

On the orders of Moray, the body was embalmed by a local surgeon in vinegar, aqua vitae, powders, odours and other necessities, dressed in sackcloth and taken to Edinburgh. There, some months later, propped up in its coffin, it heard the sentence of forfeiture passed and saw its armorial bearings struck from the Heralds' Roll, as was required by the custom of the time. Three years after the Battle of Corrichie, the Gordons returned to favour and Huntly's body was finally laid to rest in Elgin Cathedral.

AD 1420–1571

FEUDING FAMILIES

THE GORDONS OF Strathbogie were one of many great families of Aberdeenshire, Banffshire and Kincardineshire who were given their lands by King Robert the Bruce. When the stakes were high, these families would fight together for the common cause, as they had at Bannockburn and at Harlaw. However, in the absence of serious conflict, their petty rivalries and disagreements, usually over land, erupted into violence.

Many of the lairds were colourful characters, none more so than Sir Andrew de Leslie of Balquhain, north west of Aberdeen near Inverurie. He lost at least six sons on the battlefield at Harlaw; some reports claim he lost even more than six. This discrepancy may have arisen because he was said to have had seventy children, 'but most of them were unlawfully begotten'. It was reported:

> That in One Night, he begot Seven Children in sundry Places, and that all their Mothers lay in Child Bed at One Time, and that his Lady sent to every One of them in Charity Half a Boll of Meal, Half a Boll of Malt, a Wedder and Five Shillings of Money.

It was said no woman was safe from his clutches and that he carried off several 'fair maids', provoking feuds with several families, including the Forbes. Eventually, in January 1420, the Sheriff of Angus was sent to put an end to the lascivious baron's activities. Sir Andrew stood firm and at Braco, not far from his castle, fought with the Sheriff's men and was killed. Although he was not buried where he fell, his widow had a chapel built on the spot and paid a priest to say Mass for his soul every day.

The origin of the Forbes family name explains why the name is pronounced *for-bess*, rather than *forbz*, in Aberdeenshire. Tradition tells that the first to be named Forbes was a young man who had fallen in love with Bess, the daughter of a neighbouring laird on Donside. On the eve of her wedding the bride and her maidens went to wash at a hillside well, which was said to have special properties to ensure happiness and multiple children. While at the well, the bride and nine of her maidens were killed by a wild boar. The bridegroom vowed vengeance, hunted the ferocious boar and killed it near a large boulder, still known as the Boar's Stone, where it used to sharpen its tusks. As he stabbed it

THE LEGEND OF BRUX AND MUAT

———⁂———

In the 1500s the lands of Brux in Strathdon, some way west of Aberdeen, belonged to Cameron, who had a long-standing feud with Muat of Abergeldie in the Dee valley. They agreed to meet near the River Don to settle their differences, each being attended by only twelve horses. The treacherous Muat arrived with two riders on each of his twelve horses, outnumbering Cameron of Brux, who was slain along with his twelve men. His widow offered the hand of her daughter, now sole heir to the lands of Brux, to any man who would avenge her husband's death. Robert Forbes challenged Muat to a duel and killed him. The widow Brux declared that the marriage must take place and be consummated immediately, while Forbes's dirk was still wet and smelling of Muat's blood.

———⁂———

The frontispiece over the main entrance to Huntly Castle today; the Coat of Arms of the 1st Marquis of Huntly is directly above the doorway. (© Crown Copyright reproduced courtesy of Historic Scotland www.historicscotlandimages.gov.uk)

repeatedly with his dirk, he shouted 'for Bess, for Bess' – hence the name Forbes.

One of the most notorious feuds in the area was between the two most powerful families in Aberdeenshire – Forbes and Gordon – and was fuelled not only by land rivalry but also by religion. The Forbes family were staunch Protestants. The Gordons were high-profile Catholics, entrusted at the time of the Reformation with the safe-keeping of Catholic treasures from St Machar's Cathedral in Aberdeen.

It seemed as if each family was trying to outdo the other with the atrocities they inflicted, with matters coming to a head in the 1570s. The Earl of Huntly, in an attempt to lessen the rivalry between the two families, had arranged for his daughter to marry the Master of Forbes, heir to the Forbes lands. According to Gordon propaganda of the time, the master mistreated his wife causing a disagreement at a banquet at the Forbes' Druminnor Castle in 1571. By the end of the banquet twenty Gordons lay dead. A pitched battle followed nearby at Tillyangus, resulting in victory for the Gordons and the death of many Forbes

The Forbes's Corgarff Castle as it is today; the star-shaped defensive wall was added by Redcoat soldiers after 1746. (© Crown Copyright reproduced courtesy of Historic Scotland www.historic-scotlandimages.gov.uk)

men, including 'Black Arthur', the Master's brother. Prisoners were taken to Adam Gordon's castle at Auchindoun near Mortlach – present-day Dufftown. Not content with this victory, Adam Gordon pressed home his advantage, leading his men through the hills to Corgarff Castle, aiming to capture Forbes of Towie. He found the laird was absent but his wife, Margaret Campbell, was at home with her children and women servants. Margaret refused to surrender the castle and is said to have shot three Gordon men from the castle wall. Adam Gordon lost his temper and ordered that fires be set against the walls and the building be torched, murdering Margaret, her family and servants. A total of twenty-four people died in the fire that day, a massacre remembered in the ballad *Edom o' Gordon*. It is said ghostly screams have been heard in the building and that visitors to Corgarff Castle today may feel very unwelcome and a particular chill if they wear Gordon tartan.

The Master of Forbes, appointed Lieutenant of the North by the Scottish Protestant government, raised a force of 700 trained men and 100 volunteers in the south and marched to Aberdeenshire specifically to 'daunt and supress' Adam Gordon. However, Gordon received word of the approaching troops in time for him to raise a formidable force, said to be 1,500 strong, with whom he decimated the food supplies of lower Deeside to ensure the Forbes men went hungry. The two armies finally met at the Crabstane, at that time on the edge of the burgh of Aberdeen. Here, in the growing dusk, the heavily outnumbered Forbes forces were defeated by the Gordons, who succeeded

THE LAIRD WITH THE SEVEN SONS

⊸∞∞⊶

The Gordon Laird of Knock on Deeside, west of Aberdeen, had seven sons. One day, he sent them all out to cut peats for the castle's fires. Whether or not they realised, they strayed onto the neighbouring lands of Forbes of Strathgirnoc. The Forbes men were quick to attack. Not satisfied with killing the seven sons, they beheaded them and impaled their heads on their peat spades which were left standing in the peat for all to see. When the news was broken to him, the Laird of Knock was at the top of his castle's turnpike stair and, overcome, he fell down, broke his neck and died. His neighbour and relative, Gordon of Abergeldie, avenged his death by hanging Forbes of Strathgirnoc in his own castle and taking over the Forbes lands.

⊸∞∞⊶

in isolating the enemy spearsmen from the protection of their musketeers. This left them facing certain death from the Gordon bows and arrows.

It was, however, the Leslies who took local feuds to another level, directing their violence not at another family but at the citizens of Aberdeen. On the night of 1 October 1525 William Leslie, Baron of Balquhain, supported by John Leslie of Wardis, Alexander Seton of Meldrum and unnamed 'confederates and retainers', entered Aberdeen. The three lairds, described as 'potent barons in the Garioch', were there to avenge a wrong they believed had been done to them. The entire band, totalling eighty men, was armed with spears and other weapons. They furiously attacked the inhabitants in a bloody conflict in which eighty citizens, including several magistrates, were killed or wounded. Eventually, the citizens of Aberdeen fought off the raiders and drove them out of town. Following complaints to King James V, investigations were undertaken and the affair was resolved by arbitration involving both bishops and nobles. In February 1527 the two Leslie barons swore an obligation 'for themselves, their kin, friends, tenants, servants, adherents and partakers that they would not molest, vex, inquiet or trouble, the provost, bailies, council, community and inhabitants of the burgh of Aberdeen, or any one of them, in any manner or way, in time coming, in their persons, lands, or goods.' The penalty for breaching this was to be £2,000, a huge amount of money at that time. It certainly seems to have been an effective deterrent for the belligerent Leslies.

WITCHES, WARLOCKS AND SORCERY

FOR CENTURIES, SORCERY and healing were part of life in Scotland; healers were especially valued. In the 1500s the name 'witch' emerged along with the belief, perhaps taught by the Church, that these people got their powers from the Devil, arousing fear and suspicion. Using 'any manner of witchcraft, sorcery or necromancy' became a criminal act in 1563. King James VI and his bride, Anne of Denmark, became victims of witches, resulting in the king's obsession with witchcraft which inspired a frenzy of witch-hunts throughout Scotland. At its peak in 1597, eighty people were accused of witchcraft in Aberdeen alone. At least thirty were executed – strangled, then burned at the stake.

Traditionally, female witches and male warlocks were believed to meet in covens. Their cantrips (or spells) could be cast in different ways. Best known are audible curses and the malevolent look – the 'evil eye'. The shadow of a witch, coming between her victim and the sun, could cast a cantrip, or she might touch whatever or whomever she wanted to curse. Witches changed their form at will – usually into a hare, a cat or a crow; it was said warlock Colin Massie of Craiglash near Torphins could become a hare or a weasel when the occasion demanded. For more powerful cantrips a witch might use 'hackit flesh' from a dead body, a 'cursing bone', a 'pictour' or one of her own possessions. All witches' possessions were extremely dangerous – contact could cause death.

One witch, wishing ill on a neighbour, took her cursing bone and went to his croft 'between sunset and cock crow'. She grabbed the cock's favourite hen, sitting right beside him in the henhouse. Having wrung its neck, she poured its blood through the hollow bone, uttering curses.

The Warlock's Stone, Craiglash – perhaps Colin Massie cast his cantrips here. Following the witch hunts of the late 1500s the stone was broken, probably deliberately. (Author's collection)

THE WIZARD LAIRD OF SKENE

Alexander, Laird of Skene, was said never to cast a shadow. He was followed everywhere by crows, had the power to root people to the spot and was in league with the Devil.

One winter midnight, the Wizard Laird ordered his coachman to drive a special guest home. On no account was he to turn and look at his passenger. The laird told him to drive across the Loch of Skene, although there had been only one night of frost and the ice was thin. The ice held, but the temptation was too much and, just as they reached the far bank, the coachman turned to look at the stranger. There sat the horned, cloven-footed Devil himself, who immediately changed into a raven and flew off. The ice cracked and coach, horses and coachman sank to the bottom of the loch. Today, following one night of frost, it is said coach wheel tracks can be seen on the frozen surface of the loch.

The Loch of Skene, where coach wheel tracks are said to be visible in the ice following one night of frost. (Author's collection)

A pictour was made of clay or wax in the image of the intended victim, pierced with thorns or pins and then dissolved in a running stream or melted before a slow fire. Jonet Leask of Aberdeen made a wax pictour of Walter Cruickshank. Each night, she put it on a spit and turned it by her fire. As the wax melted, Walter's own body 'melted by sweating ... he took an extreme sweating with an extraordinary burning heat at his heart and liver like a fiery furnace ... and an extreme drouth and vomiting until he died.' In her purse, Helen Rogie had a pictour engraved in soft lead; a mould to make clay or wax images which she would roast at the fire.

Bewitched doorways affected the first person to pass through, giving rise to the custom of carrying a bride over the threshold of her new home to protect her from witchcraft. Margaret Ogg bewitched a byre door by cutting a witchcraft device into nine pieces and concealing them under the entrance.

Nine was the Devil's number and gave extra power to the cantrip. Ten of the farmer's twelve cows died. Isobel Cockie of Kintore cast cantrips on the doorways of Thomas Small and Alexander Harvey. Thomas contracted a fever while Alexander became fevered, was speechless for twenty-four hours and 'was never well again'. She also bewitched a neighbour's crops, which rotted and wasted away.

Infants were in particular danger. They were hidden away from the evil eye until baptised and the insides of cradles were painted a 'witch-safe' green. Crops, farm animals and their produce were also at risk; the witch was the greatest enemy of the dairy. To let her have any milk allowed her to draw away all the milk and cream from the cow. Helen Gray of Slains was found guilty of taking 'the hail substance of the mylk' from the laird's cows and ewes.

A benevolent spirit was believed to live in the rowan tree and could protect people, cattle and horses from witchcraft. Even today, many houses have a rowan on either side of the door. In earlier times, a rowanwood cross tied with red thread was hung over both house and stable doors. A similar cross was fixed to the cradle to keep a baby safe between birth and baptism. Rowan leaves might be scattered on the bed just before childbirth. Cattlemen wore sprigs of rowan, used rowan sticks for herding the beasts and tied a rowanwood and red thread cross to the tails of cows and mares following calving or foaling. Milk churns were held safely closed by a rowanwood pin. Holly and woodbine – wild honeysuckle – were also effective, but nothing surpassed the rowan.

The traditional trial of a witch or warlock was the ducking stool.

The ring in ancient St Mary's Chapel, Aberdeen, where witches were shackled while awaiting their fate. (Photo taken with kind permission of the Open Space Trust)

Immersed in a river or loch, the witch was judged innocent if she drowned and was given a Christian burial. If she survived, she was believed to be using magic, pronounced guilty and was burned at the stake. *Dowping,* carried out in Aberdeen at the harbour Quayhead, was similar; the witch was thrown into the water with a rope tied round her waist.

In 1590s Aberdeen those suspected of 'witchcraft, sorcery and other diabolical and detestable practices' were detained and tried in the Tolbooth by the Justice Court, comprising the Provost of Aberdeen, four Bailies and a jury. A *dittay,* or list of charges, was compiled. Sleep deprivation was used to extract confessions. Most of the accused were women, innocent of any wrong-doing but skilled in herbal healing, 'whose poverty, sour temper or singular habits made them an object of dislike or fear to their neighbours'. They were denounced as witches by their neighbours, friends or even family.

Fear and terror provoked by sudden, unexplained and violent illness was surely responsible for many of the charges listed in the *dittays.* Warlock Gilbert Fidlar of Auchmacoy near Ellon was accused of bewitching a pair of shoes he made for Lady Errol. The day he fitted her shoes she contracted a 'sickness in her feet and about her heart' and died. Today we would assume poorly cured leather caused a raging infection. Janet Wishart of Kintore was accused of casting her shadow on mariner Alexander Thomson while he walked to his ship, causing him to 'lay bedsick for one month'. In addition she was charged with causing, over a period of thirty years, many to suffer 'a dwining illness, melting away like ane burning candle'. She was said to have caused a neighbour's cow to produce poison rather than milk and twelve hens to fall stone dead at her feet. She was also accused, with her daughter Violet, of removing body parts for her cantrips from a hanged and putrifying body on Gallow Hill. Her son, Thomas Lees, assisted with her witchcraft and both were charged with taking part, with Isobel Cockie, in a witches' Sabbath on Hallowe'en 1595 at Aberdeen's Mercat and Fish Crosses. There, Isobel was alleged to have removed the pipe from the Devil's mouth to play the music herself while those who danced took the form of hares, 'cats or other likenesses'.

Around thirty people tried during the Aberdeen witch-hunt were *virret* (strangled) then burned to ashes at the stake. For a set fee of £1 6s 8d, the hangman would dispatch four witches in a single day. Janet Wishart and her son were sentenced to a much worse fate, 'to be brint to the deid' – they were burned alive.

Most witches were strangled and then burned to ashes. A few were burned alive. (Robert Benner Sr.)

RELIGIOUS CARNAGE

FOR 200 YEARS after the Battle of Corrichie, religion continued to cause great loss of life and bloodshed in north east Scotland. The countryside near Aberdeen was stained with the blood of Catholics, Royalists, Episcopalians, Covenanters and, later, Jacobites and government soldiers.

When the Gordons regained their power, the 6th Earl and 1st Marquis of Huntly became the natural leader of the Catholic cause. In 1594 he led the Catholics into their last action, the Battle of Glenlivet, in a remote glen midway between Aberdeen and Inverness. Gordon of Auchindoun was shot from his horse by the Royalists, who then cut off his head. Gordon of Gight was hit by three bullets and received appalling penetrating wounds when his armour sheared. Although Huntly lost some of his principal officers, he used artillery to great advantage against the superior numbers of the Royal Army. This was the first time artillery had been used in Scotland. The Royal force had never experienced shell fire before and retreated when it intensified. However, the chief of the MacLeans stood his ground and led a ferocious charge towards Huntly's standard, slaying four or five men with his Lochaber Axe. He then speared the standard-bearer's horse with the point of his axe, cut the standard-bearer in half and captured Huntly's standard. Despite these gruesome losses, Huntly won the battle.

King James VI was an advocate of tolerance and conciliation, but this battle finally provoked him into action against the Catholic rebels. Commandeering masons, tools and gunpowder in Aberdeen, he travelled to Strathbogie and personally supervised the demolition of Huntly's ornate palace. Despite being exiled, Huntly was allowed to reclaim his lands and power eighteen months later when he renounced Catholicism and was admitted into the Protestant Church.

As King of Scotland, James VI had an uneasy relationship with the Church, which he believed challenged his authority. With the Union of the Crowns in 1603 he became King James I of England, and discovered the Church of England respected him as its Supreme Governor. His attempts to impose an Anglican form of worship and church structure on the Church of Scotland created resentment and were mostly defeated by the Scottish Parliament.

In 1625 Charles I came to the throne, becoming an absentee King of Scotland based in London, as his father had been from 1603. His much-delayed Scottish coronation in 1633 was an elaborate Anglican ceremony which alienated the Presbyterian Scots. Without Parliament's support, he forced new reforms on the Church of Scotland, resulting in open rebellion. In 1638 the National Covenant was drawn up, preserving Scottish national and religious identity. Although loyal to the king, Presbyterians believed Christ, not the monarch, was head of their Church and they demanded the abolition of bishops. Thousands throughout the country signed copies of the Covenant. James Graham, 4th Earl and later 1st Marquis of Montrose, a natural leader and skilled military tactician, became their general, gaining support for civil war in Scotland from many battle-hardened Scottish mercenaries returning from Europe.

Aberdeen and the north east was fiercely Royalist and the 2nd Marquis of Huntly was appointed the King's General for the north in 1639. Undeterred that the Covenanters had been declared illegal, Montrose marched to Aberdeen at the head of an army of 9,000. The small Royalist force there was forced to withdraw and Huntly surrendered. Despite guarantees of safe conduct from Montrose, Huntly and his eldest son were arrested and imprisoned in Edinburgh Castle.

When Montrose's garrison was withdrawn from Aberdeen to deal with unexpected resistance elsewhere, Huntly's younger son, Viscount Aboyne, occupied Aberdeen for the Royalists.

Aboyne's force then marched south and encountered the well-organised Covenanters at Megray Hill near Stonehaven. Armed with Dunnottar Castle's huge siege cannons and smaller artillery pieces, they easily drove the Royalists back towards Aberdeen, pursuing them in great numbers and bringing with them their heavy artillery. When Aboyne reached the Bridge of Dee he had only a small force remaining for the defence of the bridge and its gatehouse. The bridge was of vital importance, as the Dee, swollen with midsummer rain, was impossible to ford.

Early next morning, 18 June, the Covenanters attacked with the firepower of their massive cannons, dislodging huge chunks of masonry from the gatehouse and bridge. Their musket fire was less accurate, causing only one Royalist death and one injury. Despite Aboyne's inferior firepower, his defences held. Attempts to storm the bridge were repulsed. After dark, Montrose moved his cannons closer. Next morning the Royalist force was depleted when many men left to attend the funeral

The Bridge of Dee, Aberdeen, as it is today. (Author's collection)

of the prominent supporter who had been killed the previous day. This gave Montrose the opportunity he needed. A few Covenanter horsemen drew the entire Royalist cavalry up-river, leaving only a skeleton force to defend the bridge. Bombarding it with accurate cannon fire, Montrose then turned his artillery on the cavalry. John Seton, laird of Pitmedden was blown in half by the full force of one shell. Colonel Johnstone, an experienced Royalist officer, was injured and partly buried by a demolished wall. Seeing the Covenanters storming towards the bridge, he gave the order to retire. Ironically, neither side was aware that the Berwick peace treaty had been signed before the Battle of the Bridge of Dee had even begun.

For most of the next five years, Aberdeen was garrisoned by Covenanter troops. Meanwhile, the Marquis of Montrose became disillusioned with the extremist Covenanters, changed allegiance and effectively restarted civil war on the Royalists' behalf in 1644. With a combined force of Irish Catholics and Highlanders, he marched north and crossed the Dee to the west of

The Marquis of Montrose statue, Montrose. (Author's collection)

Aberdeen. Montrose sent a herald and a drummer boy into the burgh with a note requesting surrender. The Provost, closely watched by Covenanter officers, was powerless to comply. Montrose

THE INCOMPETENT COLONEL GUNN

To compensate for Aboyne's youth and inexperience, the king assigned a military adviser to him. Colonel Gunn, however, did not prove his worth. At Megray Hill, he insisted on breakfast before meeting the Covenanter Army. Battle-hardened Colonel Johnstone had to interrupt to ask permission to engage the enemy; Colonel Gunn authorised this but continued his breakfast. At the Bridge of Dee, it was Gunn who ordered the entire Royalist cavalry up-river, despite the river being too high to ford. After the battle, he reported directly to the king in Berwick that he had single-handedly led 300 Royalists to victory over the Covenanters, shooting holes in Montrose's hat.

was infuriated when a Covenanter musketeer shot the drummer boy dead as he returned to the Royalist lines.

The Denburn, crossed by only the Bow Brig, formed Aberdeen's natural western boundary. On a dull, damp autumn day the Battle of Justice Mills was fought in the oat fields by the mills, on the approach to the bridge. Heavily outnumbered by the Covenanters, the small but experienced Royalist force was led by officers who understood battle tactics. The Covenanters' cannons roared but the wind blew the smoke back in their faces, temporarily blinding them. Their cavalry attacks were fragmented and uncoordinated. Footsoldiers attempted to outflank Montrose but were held back by sustained musket fire and overpowered when reinforcements arrived from the opposite Royalist flank. Covenanter cavalry charged at the Royalist centre, which parted to let them through, allowing Montrose's well-disciplined footsoldiers to open up raging musket fire on the cavalry's back. Montrose's Highlanders and Irish troops pressed home the attack, their claymores slicing easily through wooden pikes and human flesh. The bloodbath resulted in panic and the Covenanters fled. Justice Mill Lane and the Hardgate in Aberdeen city centre now cover the battlefield.

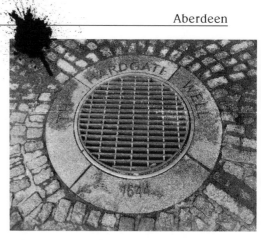

Following the Battle of Justice Mills, so many washed their wounds at the Hardgate Well that it ran red with blood. (Author's collection)

On the day of the battle, so many injured washed their wounds at the Hardgate Well that it ran red with blood.

Montrose had promised his brutish troops that they could sack Aberdeen. Their entrance into the town was barbaric, hacking down every man they encountered. They stripped the best-dressed victims before stabbing them so the clothes would not be soiled. Women were seized and raped in the street. On seeing the evidence, Montrose was appalled by the force he had unleashed on Aberdeen's residents.

Montrose and his Royalists left Aberdeen having learned that a large Covenanter force was rapidly approaching. The Covenanters reoccupied the burgh only two days later.

THE GREAT PESTILENCE!

OVER THE CENTURIES, Aberdeen's citizens have endured leprosy, cholera, smallpox, dysentery and, more recently, typhoid. However, it was Plague which had the greatest effect on the burgh, stopping trade, council meetings, court cases and church services. In the 1647 epidemic, it killed a fifth of the population in just seven months.

Great Pestilence, Plague or Black Death is a horrific disease whichever name it is given. Caused by the micro-organism *Yersinia pestis*, it is spread by fleas. One bite from an infected flea transfers up to 24,000 *Yersinia pestis* bacilli into an animal or human host. In humans, symptoms appear two to six days later. These include high fevers, chills, headaches, total exhaustion, vomiting and extremely tender lymph glands which swell to the size of an egg. These swellings, called buboes, are hot, suppurate and bleed, and are usually found in the groin, neck and armpits. From each ten people infected and not treated, between six and eight will die, usually within three to seven days. This is Bubonic Plague and would have been the type of Pestilence to affect Aberdeen's citizens, spread by flea-infected animals, particularly rats. Some of those infected may have developed secondary pneumonic or septicaemic plague. Left untreated, these very virulent forms of the disease kill virtually everyone. The higher proportion of survivors in Aberdeen indicates that these forms of Plague would not have been the primary source of infection.

Plague still exists today and affects animals and humans in a wide range of countries in Africa, Asia and South and North America, particularly the western USA. *Yersinia pestis* is a bacterium, and therefore early treatment with antibiotics is usually successful. Nowadays it is still a horrific disease – in 1500s and 1600s Aberdeen, with no treatment available, it must have been absolutely terrifying.

In 1497, James IV endowed Aberdeen's King's College with the first Chair of Medicine in the English-speaking world. The first to hold the post was James Cumming, who was also appointed burgh physician to 'visit the sick and show them his medicine'. Aberdeen was therefore better prepared than most towns to deal with Plague. Before the appointment of Cumming, there were only three medical practitioners to serve the burgh and most people would have relied on barber-surgeons for medical treatment, usually blood-letting. There was already an understanding of how diseases were spread; for example, as early as the 1200s, lepers were not permitted to attend Mass in church. The 'Great Pox', a form of syphilis, had been successfully held at bay in the 1490s and it seems strict regulations may have kept Aberdeen's population free of Plague until the early 1500s.

The fear of disease had led to the magistrates and council developing preventative measures, which included guarding the burgh gates and restricting the movement of people through them. No outsiders were to be given lodgings and anyone falling ill – regardless of symptoms – had to remain in their house, receiving no visitors. Sailors who were ill or had come from suspect ports were quarantined in the blockhouse at Pocra Quay and their goods were burned. In 1512, Pestilence was rife in Edinburgh but it was not until a

year later that Aberdeen Council implemented preventative regulations. These were less comprehensive than before and with no specific order to close or guard the burgh gates, the inevitable soon happened.

By April 1514, Plague was ravaging Aberdeen, perhaps for the first time. Beggars were banished and visitors' identities had to be reported to the council; their hosts had to vouch they were free of Plague. Shared entries and passages were secured and houses searched for victims. Perhaps on Cumming's advice, the importance of cleansing goods and quarantining sufferers was recognised. Those who were ill were sealed up in their houses to die or recover. Punishment for non-compliance was severe: four people were banished from the burgh for burying a man who 'died in the pestilence' in a communal midden. In a later outbreak, residents were burned on the hand for contravening anti-Plague measures. Beggars and vagabonds who

PLAGUE SUPERSTITIONS

Some believed that sin opened the pores and allowed the Pestilence to enter the body. Others blamed Jews, whom they thought had poisoned wells, and in the 1300s there were mass burnings of Jews in Europe. In some countries, earthquakes were blamed. One Aberdeen victim was fined for seeking relief of his fevers by charming – witchcraft! Many believed that a cock or hen held next to a bubo would draw out the infection. Others thought wearing a ring of stone on the third finger of the left hand – believed to connect with the heart – would prevent infection. Winter was thought to kill off the disease with fewer cases in cold weather. This could be due to people travelling less in winter, but it is more likely the cold weather killed the fleas which spread Plague. In Aberdeen some believed Pestilence was caused by leading sinful lives – salmon fishermen were asked not to fish on Sundays and the Council cracked down on the burgh's 'whoredoms and abominations'.

The Dance of Death procession. (Thomas Fisher Rare Book Library, University of Toronto)

resisted expulsion were branded on the cheek with a hot iron. A father was punished for concealing his ill baby, although the child did not have Plague.

By the time Plague returned to Scotland in 1644, Aberdeen had been ravaged by the Civil War, lost many of its merchants and poor summer weather had led to crop failure. Plague spread north from Edinburgh, into Peterhead then to Inverbervie, surrounding the burgh and getting closer all the time. Armed guards were posted at the Bridge of Dee and at the Blockhouse. The port was closed and merchants were prohibited from buying cloth from the hinterland. But after a time the guard became lax, with masters delegating their servants to keep the watch.

A woman travelled from Plague-ridden Brechin to Pitmuckstone, now known as Pitstruan in Aberdeen's West End. Then a child from Pitmuckstone was allowed into the burgh to attend school, carrying Pestilence into Aberdeen. A new watch was appointed; neglect of duties incurred a £100 fine. Poison was laid for mice and rats, and middens were

cleared from streets and shared entries. No one was allowed to leave or enter the burgh. Camps with huts for ill people were built beyond the town gates on the Links and at Woolmanhill. Sending a family member there was effectively a death sentence so many of the ill were concealed. The council decreed anyone harbouring a Plague suspect would face the death penalty and a standing gibbet was erected in the Castlegate. Plague devastated Aberdeen and normal life stopped. An official cleanser was appointed to burn or boil infected goods; sheer volume meant he very soon required an assistant. Suspect goods had to be washed nightly and exposed to the frosty air. Residents had to endure house searches aimed at finding the ill; the searchers also buried the dead from the huts. By the end of 1647, 1,600 people had died since the epidemic

Child's Dance of Death. (Thomas Fisher Rare Book Library, University of Toronto)

started in May. Worst affected were the poor, particularly the young and the old. Most were buried in mass graves, 37,000 turves being cut on the Links to cover these. In recent times, bones and skeletons have been found during development work near the harbour.

But not all victims died. Those who recovered were ordered to cleanse their clothes and goods and remain in quarantine for forty days in the huts, followed by fifteen days in their own homes before they were allowed to attend church, markets or other gatherings. In addition they had to carry a white stick for twenty days so that other citizens could identify and avoid them. Perhaps these extreme measures, together with the harsh winters, led to Aberdeen faring much better than other burghs. Only one in five of its population died in 1647, although in the following years the council did actively seek new residents from the country to take up positions as craftsmen and servants to replace those who had died. Other towns lost three in five, and more, of their citizens. Across the North Sea, Norway effectively lost its independence after the Black Death killed 60 per cent of its entire population, including most in government, resulting in union with Denmark in 1380.

DUNNOTTAR CASTLE AND THE CROWN JEWELS

THE SHOCKWAVES FROM Charles I's trial and execution in 1649 were felt throughout Scotland, not least in the traditionally Royalist burgh of Aberdeen. A Declaration read at the Mercat Cross in the Castlegate reported the king's death and proclaimed his son King Charles II of Scotland. Support for the new king inflamed Cromwell, who sent his army north to Dunnottar Castle, south of Aberdeen, to seize and destroy the Scottish Crown Jewels.

Royalists and Covenanters each occupied Aberdeen for short periods following the Battle of Justice Mills in 1644. Each saw the town as an excellent source of revenue. The 1647 Plague epidemic had left Aberdonians exhausted and demoralised and the town played no major role in either the eventual victory of the Covenanters or in Scotland's involvement in the English Civil War. In 1651 the impoverished burgh was unable to pay the levy required by Cromwell's General Monck. He and his men treated the town and its residents well and he did not insist on payment. His officers funded a new building for King's College, still called The Cromwell Tower today.

Despite both James VI and Charles I being absentee kings, Aberdonians felt great affection for them, particularly for Charles who had spent part of his childhood in Aberdeenshire at Fyvie Castle. They were therefore shocked and appalled when he was condemned to death by Cromwell's English court. The people of Scotland were utterly outraged that he was beheaded without any consultation with the Scottish Parliament. The Marquis of Huntly, a staunch Royalist, was executed shortly afterwards. In 1650 the Marquis of Montrose, with a force of European mercenaries, attempted to raise support for the new King Charles II but was defeated by the Covenanter Army. Montrose was executed and part of his dismembered body – the right hand and forearm – was nailed to the Tolbooth in Aberdeen as a deterrent to others.

Charles I's son, having reached agreement with the Presbyterian Scottish Parliament, was proclaimed King Charles II of Scotland. He landed at Speymouth in Moray in June 1650 and travelled to Aberdeen where he was given the silver keys of the burgh. But Cromwell's Army was on its way north to subdue the Scots and destroyed

THE HONOURS OF SCOTLAND

The Honours, or Regalia, are the Sword of State, Sceptre and Crown. The silver-gilt Sceptre was presented to King James IV in 1494 by Pope Alexander VI as a mark of Papal support for Scotland. The Sword of State was a gift to James IV from Pope Julius II in 1507. It has a heavily decorated silver-gilt handle and intricately engraved blade. The Crown, remodelled from an earlier crown for James V in 1540, has a circlet of Scottish gold encrusted with precious stones, gems and Scottish freshwater pearls. The Honours were used together for the first time in 1543 at the coronation of the infant Mary, Queen of Scots at Stirling Castle.

The Honours owe their continued existence to many loyal Scots, some known, others unknown. They are the oldest Crown Jewels in the UK and among the oldest in Christendom. When the monarchy was restored in 1660 they were returned to Edinburgh Castle; in 1707 following the Act of Union with England, they were locked away in

The Crown, Sceptre and Sword of State – the Honours of Scotland. (© Crown Copyright reproduced courtesy of Historic Scotland www.historicscotlandimages.gov.uk)

an oak chest. In 1818, Sir Walter Scott obtained permission to have the chest opened and found the Honours exactly as they had been left 111 years previously.

The Honours are on display in Edinburgh Castle together with the Stone of Destiny, returned to Scotland in 1996, 700 years after 'The Hammer of the Scots' had taken it south. Since 1999, the Crown has been present at the official opening of each session of the new Scottish Parliament.

the Covenanter Army at Dunbar a few months later.

On New Year's Day 1651, Charles was crowned King of Scotland at Scone with the full Scottish Regalia. This infuriated Cromwell, who had already destroyed the English Regalia; the jewels had been sold and the precious metals melted to be made into coins. Cromwell was determined that the Scottish Regalia would suffer the same fate.

Following the coronation and after Edinburgh Castle fell to Cromwell's army, the Scottish Parliament ordered that the Honours, together with the king's private papers, be taken to the Earl Marischal's Dunnottar Castle for safekeeping. The Earl Marischal, imprisoned by Cromwell in the Tower of London, appointed accomplished soldier George Ogilvy of Barras Governor of Dunnottar Castle. Ogilvy garrisoned the Castle with sixty-nine local men, many fewer than he would have wished.

Cromwell's army arrived at Dunnottar in early September and found the castle could not be stormed due to its unique defensive position on a much-eroded clifftop promontory. Until heavy artillery could be brought north, the only option was a siege. The castle garrison survived by bringing in supplies by small boat under cover of darkness. Dunnottar Castle was the only place in Scotland still flying the royal flag when, in May 1652, Cromwell's heavy cannons finally arrived. The first bombardment hit the Great Tower with twelve shells, killing seven men and depleting the garrison. 'The havock of bombs and the shoaks of thundering cannon' continued for ten days. On 24 May 1652, following eight months of siege, Ogilvy surrendered 'with all the honours of war'. However, Cromwell's Commander, Major General Morgan, was disappointed when he and his men searched the castle, for the king's papers and the Honours of Scotland were nowhere to be found. In their fury, Morgan's men demolished the chapel and damaged the countess's suite. Ogilvy and his wife were imprisoned in the castle but refused to reveal the secret. Mrs Ogilvy died from the effects of her ill-treatment.

WHERE WERE THE CROWN JEWELS?

Almost two months before the siege ended, Christian Fletcher, wife of the Revd James Grainger of nearby Kinneff Kirk, had been granted General Morgan's permission to visit her friend Mrs Ogilvy in the castle. On leaving the castle, she

---

Reporting to the Countess Marischal on 31 March 1652, the Revd James Grainger wrote:

I, Mr James Grainger, minister at Kinneff, grant me to have in my custody the Honours of the Kingdom viz., the Crown, Sceptre and Sword. For the Crown and Sceptre I raised the pavement stone just before the pulpit, in the night tyme and digged under it one hole and put them in there and filled up the hole and layed down the stone just as it was before and removed the mould that remained so that none would have discerned the stone to have been raised at all.

The Sword again, at the west end of the church, among the common soil that stand there, I digged down in the ground betwixt the twa foremost of these rails and laid it down within the case of it and covered it up, as that removing the superfluous mould it could not be discerned by anybody for it shall please God to call me by death before they be called for, your Ladyship will find them in that place.

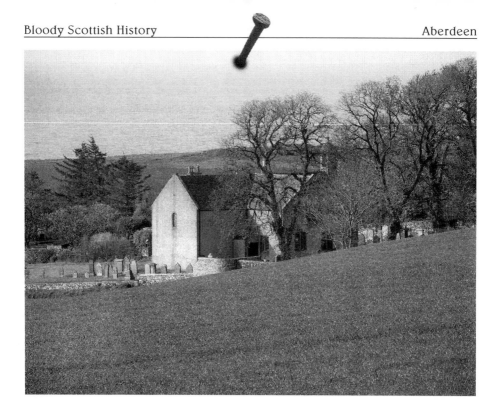

Kinneff Old Kirk, where the Honours of Scotland were buried under the floor in 1651; the church as it is today. (Author's collection)

had the Royal Crown, weighing 1.64kg, hidden in her lap under her dress. Her maid carried out the Sword and Sceptre in a bag of flax on her back. Nearly 1.4 metres long, the Sword had to be broken to fit the sack – today the signs of repair are very visible. They did not take the sword belt, which was found by one of Ogilvy's descendants in 1790, built into the garden wall of Barras Castle. It is said that General Morgan himself assisted Mrs Grainger to mount her horse before she and her maid rode the few miles south to Kinneff. That night, she and her husband slept with the Crown, Sword and Sceptre hidden at the bottom of their bed. Thereafter the Honours were buried under the floor in the church where they remained until 1660 when the monarchy was restored. At the opening of the Scottish Parliament in 1661, the Earl Marischal carried the Crown while his brothers bore the Sceptre and Sword.

THE KING O'ER THE WATER

THE ROMANTIC IMAGES of the poems, songs, novels and paintings inspired by the Jacobite period are very far from the reality. This was a bitterly fought and bloody rebellion lasting from 1689 until 1746. It was effectively a civil war, with the government and most Protestants, including many Scots, fighting against the supporters of the Royal House of Stuart. The latter were mainly Catholics, Episcopalians and Scots, but also included some English and Irish. Many lairds from Aberdeen and its hinterland were closely involved in plotting the 1715 Rising. Other landowners and many Aberdonians supported the 1745 Rebellion.

In 1685 James VII and II succeeded his brother Charles II. James was a Catholic convert and extremely unpopular. In 1688, the birth and baptism of his son, a Catholic heir, also named James, forced both Scottish and English Parliaments to take action and the king fled to France. Both governments invited his daughter Mary to rule jointly with her staunchly-Protestant husband William. James's younger daughter Anne succeeded them in 1702. Queen Anne wholeheartedly supported the Act of Union of 1707, which brought England and Scotland

JACOBITE SYMBOLS AND NICKNAMES

James VII's supporters took the name Jacobite from the Latin form of his name, *Jacobus*. Their support had to be covert, leading to nicknames and symbols which allowed loyal Jacobites to recognise each other. They would secretly drink James's health by passing their glass over a water jug or fingerbowl during the loyal toast – drinking to the king o'er the water in exile in France. His son was 'The Chevalier' as he had fought for Louis XIV under the name Chevalier de Saint Georges; the Government knew him as The Pretender to the throne. His supporters wore the wild white rose. The first Jacobite leader was James Grahame of Claverhouse, Bonnie Dundee, who was killed in battle at Killiecrankie in 1689. King George was 'The Wee German Lairdie'. The Earl of Mar, John Erskine, who had supported the 1707 Union but later changed allegiance, was known as Bobbin' Jock.

The Mercat Cross, Aberdeen, where The Old Pretender was proclaimed King James VIII and III. (Author's collection)

together as one country, Great Britain. On her death, the obvious heir was her half-brother, James, but as a Catholic he was not acceptable to Parliament. The closest Protestant heir was James VI and I's great-grandson, the German Elector of Hanover, who became King George I in 1714.

The Earl of Mar led the plan to restore a Stuart King to the throne of Great Britain. In his castle at Kildrummy in remote Strathdon, he hosted meetings with landowners, including the Earl Marischal, George Keith, to hatch a plot to oust George I and proclaim 'The Chevalier' King James VIII and III. They marched to Corgarff Castle where they armed themselves before continuing to Braemar. On the pretext of a deer hunt, senior Jacobites congregated and made their final plans at John Farquharson's Invercauld House. On 6 September 1715 they raised the Jacobite Standard nearby at Braemar. A fortnight later, the Earl Marischal and other Jacobite lords rode into Aberdeen with swords drawn,

ready for action. At the Mercat Cross in the Castlegate they proclaimed James Francis Edward Stuart, King James VIII and III.

Very soon the Jacobite Army was 12,000 strong, including many men from Aberdeen and its hinterland, and academic staff and students from both King's and Marischal Colleges. In November both sides claimed victory at the Battle of Sheriffmuir but it was the Jacobites who retreated. Mar was not a good military Commander and it soon became clear that the Jacobites needed an effective leader – their king. But James was far from Scotland, still 'o'er the water'. The death of Louis XIV in early September also deprived the Jacobites of the French assistance they desperately needed. In December, James landed in safe Keith territory at Peterhead, rendezvoused with Earl Marischal George Keith at Newburgh then travelled south to Aberdeen and the Keiths' castle at Stonehaven, where supporters were waiting. James held

Court at Scone over the New Year but the planned coronation did not take place. He was not the inspiring leader the Jacobites had hoped he would be. They withdrew north and, only a few weeks after his arrival, James left from Montrose with the Earl of Mar, bound for France. Government forces arrived in Aberdeen in February 1716 and found no resistance. The Rising of 1715 was over. Jacobite supporters lost everything. Castles were burned. Properties and possessions were forfeit to the government and sold. Once-powerful families fled into exile.

The old hopes lingered on. In 1743 James VIII and III proclaimed his son, Charles Edward Stuart, Regent. Charles was a natural, charismatic leader. His confidence was infectious and he inspired devotion. Despite arriving in the Hebrides in 1745 with only seven companions he soon had considerable support. In and around Aberdeen, this included two elderly influential lairds, Lord Pitsligo and John Gordon of Glenbuchat, as well as younger Farquharsons, Burnetts, Gordons, Inneses, Irvines, MacGregors, Menzies and Duguids.

In September 1745, James VIII and III was again proclaimed King at the Castlegate in Aberdeen, albeit less efficiently than thirty years previously. His supporters were locked out of the Mercat Cross so an armed party was sent for the Provost and the keys. Prince Charles and his army marched south into England. Finding no resistance but no real support, they turned back after reaching Derby. Around Aberdeen, Jacobites alienated many when they threatened to burn homes and farms if owners did not join their campaign.

SYMBOLS AND NICKNAMES OF THE '45

Charles was The Young Chevalier and The Young Pretender; his father became The Old Pretender. Charles was an attractive young man and became known as Bonnie Prince Charlie. A rose with two rosebuds symbolised James VIII and III and his heirs Charles and Henry. The white cockade, made from white ribbon, derived from the wild white rose worn in 1715. The oak leaf and acorns had been associated with the Stuarts since Charles II's time. The butterfly symbolised the hope of the Stuarts' return from exile. The sunflower turns to follow the sun like a loyal follower. The Medusa head was also a secret sign, signifying protector or guardian.

Bonnie Prince Charlie, age twelve. (Photo taken with kind permission of Blairs Museum Trust)

Occasionally, these threats were carried out. Government supporters in Aberdeen requested help and a detachment marched from Inverness, arriving at Inverurie, 17 miles north west of Aberdeen, a few days before Christmas.

The government Commanders believed the Jacobites in Aberdeen, together with recently arrived French reinforcements, would march south to meet their prince. Overconfident, they posted no sentries and billeted some of their men outside Inverurie. They were therefore shocked when Jacobites appeared at the unguarded fords on Inverurie's two rivers, the Don and the Urie. Despite coming under sporadic fire, the rebels soon forded the freezing water and advanced on the government troops, opening up with sustained fire. Within twenty minutes, Inverurie was under Jacobite control.

The rebels left Aberdeen in January 1746 to join the prince, leaving no military garrison. Towards the end of February, the Duke of Cumberland, George II's son, arrived with twenty-one regiments of Redcoats. He was welcomed and installed in what is now Provost Skene's House. His men commandeered the recently-completed, unoccupied Robert Gordon's Hospital and their horses were stabled in the West Church of St Nicholas, derelict at the time. Five weeks later Cumberland and his forces moved north in pursuit of the Jacobites. On 16 April 1746, the Jacobite cause died on Culloden Moor north west of Aberdeen near Inverness. Outnumbered almost two-to-one, the Jacobites were slaughtered by 'Butcher Cumberland'

Invercauld House, as it is today; here plans for the 1715 Rising were finalised (not open to the public). (Author's collection)

and his Redcoats. The battle lasted just forty minutes.

Reprisals were brutal. Homes of Jacobite supporters were plundered and burned. One Jacobite, Alexander Irvine, was lucky to escape from Culloden. At his home, Drum Castle just west of Aberdeen, he hid in a secret room while his sister distracted the search party of Redcoats. He escaped to exile in Paris; others also travelled overseas to France, Scandinavia, North America or India. Jacobites risked their lives to ensure the Bonnie Prince also escaped. The Redcoats occupied castles in strategic positions, including Braemar and Corgarff. From these, they kept the Highlands peaceful and enforced the strict new regulations which outlawed speaking Gaelic, playing bagpipes and wearing clan tartans.

CRIME AND PUNISHMENT

At Least for Some

VALUES **WERE VERY** different in the 1700s and 1800s. Stealing livestock was a capital offence; the theft of a single animal resulted in hanging. A seventeen-year-old who stole thirty sheep was executed, despite pleas for leniency. Housebreaking and pickpocketing were punished by public whipping, imprisonment, banishment or transportation.

In the 1830s the Coutts brothers of Aberdeen, found guilty of housebreaking, were imprisoned; George, aged sixteen, for twelve months and John, aged just eleven, for eighteen months. A second conviction for housebreaking led to George being transported for fourteen years to Van Diemen's Land, now Tasmania. The following year, John was tried for 'theft, habit and repute' and also transported to Van Diemen's Land. He was only fourteen when transported and died less than four years later. George received a ticket of leave in 1844 and later a conditional pardon.

Wife assault was punished with a 'whipping through the streets'. The typical sentence for assault with intent to ravish was whipping through the streets and banishment to 'the plantations' for life. In 1756 Christian Clark of Fraserburgh was charged with keeping a bawdy house, entertaining men 'in the night-time... and sailors upon Sundays'. She was banished from Aberdeenshire for life. In 1815 The White Ship, a house of ill repute in Aberdeen, was attacked by a mob of over 500 which broke in, made a bonfire of the contents and

Prisoners and those who had signed their indentures were locked up in the Tolbooth's cells. (Author's collection)

The spiral staircase and tiny windows prevented escape. (Author's collection)

'maltreated the faces of the backsliding young women inside'. The military was required to restore order. Two of the mob were imprisoned for twelve months; their leader was transported for seven years.

In 1762, Doctor Thomas Benzie was charged with being a Quack Doctor. In Aberdeen Infirmary he had cut a cancerous growth from a patient's lip. Magistrates found he had 'greatly spoiled the ... lip by ignorantly cutting the same'. He was prohibited from practising and would be banished and publicly disgraced if he did not comply. By order of the court, his sentence was published in the *Aberdeen Journal*; his name appeared in very large capitals. Concealing pregnancy and 'procuring abortion' were also severely punished. Doctor Philp of Huntly stood trial in 1771 for performing a 'violent operation in order to deliver Elizabeth Ray at the time that she was 14 weeks pregnant'. He was transported for life to the plantations.

In 1700s England, stealing a child was not an offence; the only charge applicable was theft of the child's clothes. Scottish Law was very different as here child stealing was punished by execution. In 1784 servant Margaret Irvine stole her Edinburgh employers' three-year-old son and exploited him for begging in Aberdeen for twelve months. Although the boy had not been harmed she was sentenced to be hanged. This was later reduced to transportation. Similar crimes were given the same sentence but the Aberdeen merchants trading in child slaves were never charged.

In the mid-1700s, to escape poverty, the law or the Redcoats in the aftermath of Culloden, many adults 'sold their indentures' – they were given money in return for an agreed number of years of their lives, working as servants in America. They had to swear before a magistrate that they were doing so voluntarily. On arrival in Philadelphia they were sold to the highest bidder, usually a plantation owner. This was legal trade but they travelled in appalling conditions.

Not all were indentured voluntarily. Some people sold their wives, brothers, sisters or older children for a shilling. Many well-respected Aberdeen businessmen took part in illegal operations to supplement the numbers of indentured servants they exported. Children, some as young as seven, were kidnapped and kept prisoner until space could be found on a ship. These merchants employed pipers to play for the children, not to entertain them but to drown out their screams and sobs. Although it was common knowledge in Aberdeen that this was happening, no one tried to help because those behind the abhorrent trade included the Town Clerk, baillies and magistrates. Around 600 young boys and girls

were kidnapped and sent abroad from Aberdeen between 1740 and 1746.

James Ingram, aged twelve, was snatched as he ran an errand for his mother in Aberdeen. When she went to the shop of the merchant she believed had taken him, she was forcibly ejected. Later, she saw her son in chapel and took him home. A few nights later four ruffians came for the boy, claimed he was legally indentured and took the crying chid away. The Ingrams managed to find an honest magistrate who ordered that the boy should be returned to them.

The Jamiesons of Oldmeldrum were not so lucky when their ten-year-old son John disappeared from home. Challenging the merchant whom he believed had taken his son, Mr Jamieson was told that John, despite his being 'under the age of pupillarity', had made a legal agreement with him. Mr Jamieson searched and found John being exercised at Aberdeen shore with around sixty other children, guarded by a man armed with a horsewhip who prevented Mr Jamieson from rescuing

BIZARRE CRIMES

The period's more unusual crimes give an insight into life at the time. In 1765 John MacGhee, vintner in Aberdeen, was fined £5 for failing to give lodging to strangers – his crime was 'inhospitality'. Gideon Duncan of Old Aberdeen was charged in 1753 with disturbing the congregation in church by deliberately singing out of tune.

Gideon had a good strong voice and had been taught the recently introduced new psalm tunes which the Professors of King's College supported. Despite the trained singers' best efforts, the rest of the congregation continued to sing in the old lugubrious style. Gideon, upset by the resulting cacophony, 'planted himself in the body of the church' and sang, loudly, in the old manner, creating 'a tumult in the Church'. The magistrate, a Professor at King's College, fined Gideon £50 plus expenses and imprisoned him until the fine was paid.

Peter Williamson may have shared a cell with characters like these. (Author's collection)

him. Seeking legal help, he discovered it would be pointless to ask a magistrate to order his son to be freed; many magistrates 'had a hand in those doings'. He was also threatened that anyone who complained would himself be sent away.

In 1743, Peter Williamson, the twelve-year-old son of a farmer near Aboyne, was snatched while staying with an aunt in Aberdeen. Despite his father's and brother's determined search, he was transferred to the hold of a ship for the passage to America. Seasickness, disease and poor sanitation made conditions appalling for the forty people crammed into the hold. Children, including many younger than Peter, cried constantly and screamed in terror when the ship ran aground off the shore of America. In Philadelphia, Peter was bought by a kind Scottish master who agreed to educate him in return for an additional year's indenture. When he died a few years later, he left Peter money

and his freedom. Following an eventful period in America, Peter returned to Britain, where the book he wrote about his experiences was published. On his return to Aberdeen in 1758, the magistrates and baillies were incensed by the contents of his 'pamphlet'. Following a sham trial, he was imprisoned in the Tolbooth; the offending pages of the book were burned in public by the 'common hangman'. After serving his sentence and moving to Edinburgh, Peter brought legal proceedings against the Town Clerk, merchants and others involved in his kidnapping and enforced indenture. Those accused made counter-allegations, tried to prevent the action being raised, attempted to settle out of court and to influence the judge, all to no avail. In 1768 Peter was awarded £200 damages plus 100 guineas costs; huge amounts at that time. The Aberdeen slavers were exposed. For once, justice was done.

THE FINEST REGIMENT IN THE WORLD

FOR 200 YEARS, the Gordon Highlanders have been part of Aberdeen's history. Ordinary men from the burgh and its hinterland – farmers, fishermen, gamekeepers, tradesmen, academics and students – signed up. Sons followed their fathers and grandfathers into the Gordons' regimental family. They served in distant lands, but their roots were firmly in north east Scotland. They earned a reputation for professionalism, courage and success, often in dangerous and difficult circumstances. Their motto *Bydand* means 'steadfast'. Witnessing their actions during the Boer War, the young journalist Winston Churchill, later Prime Minister, said, 'There is no doubt they are the finest regiment in the world.'

For centuries the Gordon nobility, supported by their family and tenants, had fought bravely, first for their religion and later for their king. In the social unrest and uncertainty of the late 1700s, post-revolutionary France was seen as a real threat to Britain. The Army desperately needed more men. The reward for signing up was 'the King's shilling'; soldiers were also paid a shilling a day, six times what tradesmen earned. In 1794, the 4th Duke of Gordon responded to King George III's request to raise a regiment. However, neither the King's shilling nor clan loyalty were sufficient persuasion until the stunningly beautiful Duchess of Gordon lent her support.

Jean Gordon, known as the Duchess Jean, was a forthright and outspoken woman, centuries before her time.

Painting of the Duchess Jean recruiting for the Gordons' new regiment. (The Gordon Highlanders' Museum, Aberdeen)

She gave birth to their son shortly before the Duke's mistress, also Jean, had a son; both boys were named George. The Duchess's reaction was to refer to the illegitimate son as 'the Duke's George' and to her own son as 'my George'. By 1794 the Duchess's George, the Marquess of Huntly, was already a Lieutenant Colonel and became the new regiment's first commanding officer. His mother was determined his regiment should be successful and toured local town fairs and markets with her daughters. It is said she rewarded recruits not only with the king's shilling, but also with a kiss; sometimes she would have a golden guinea between her lips. On 24 June 1794, the new regiment, officially the 100th Regiment of Foot, paraded in Aberdeen. Next day, the 100th sailed for Southampton and four years of garrison duty in the Mediterranean. In 1799 (now renamed the 92nd) they had a baptism of fire, fighting the French at Egmont-op-Zee in the Netherlands. Their Commander, George Gordon, was badly wounded. Two years later, they were back in action against the French in Egypt.

It was in the Peninsular War that the 92nd earned their reputation as one of the most dependable units in the British Army. In 1809, they fought in Spain under Sir John Moore at Corunna. Ever since then, his death has been commemorated by black threads in uniform shoulder cords and black buttons, rather than white, on the spats. In keeping with Highland tradition, the regiment was always led into battle by its pipers. In 1813, the regiment fought ferociously to push back the French from the River Nive in the Pyrenees. When the

Drawing of the Gordon Highlanders' cap badge. (The Gordon Highlanders' Museum, Aberdeen)

piper was killed another took his place; when he too was killed, a third stepped forward and played to rouse the soldiers' battle lust. The French fell back and the British crossed into France.

However, the legend of the 92nd really dates from 1815. They marched 18 miles from Brussels to Quatre Bras where, heavily outnumbered, they fought for five hours. The indecisive battle cost them dearly; almost half were killed or wounded, including twenty-five of their thirty-six officers. Just two days later, a much-depleted force of 300 was concealed on high ground at Waterloo. As the 3,000-strong French column advanced, the 92nd was ordered to charge. At the same time, the Royal Scots Greys cavalry was also told to charge. In the confusion which resulted, the men of the 92nd grabbed hold of the stirrups and legs of the passing cavalrymen, charging forward together with the cry

'Scotland forever', lopping off heads and putting their bayonets to good use. The stunned French fell back, their advance stopped in its tracks.

In 1880, during the Second Afghan War, the 92nd took part in the twenty-three-day, 320-mile march from Kabul to relieve the siege of Kandahar, crossing rugged mountains in appalling conditions. In 1881 the 92nd amalgamated with the 75th Stirlingshire Regiment to become the Gordon Highlanders. The same year, in a precursor to the war twenty years later, a small detachment took part in an indecisive battle against the Boers in South Africa.

On 20 October 1897, on the North West Frontier between India and Afghanistan, the Gordon Highlanders fought what was to become their most famous action. Enemy Afridi tribesmen held the rocky heights around the village of Dargai. British troops had to cross 150 metres of open ground, raked by enemy fire, to reach the bottom of the steep 200-metre climb to the enemy-held ridge. The tribesmen withstood repeated attacks by three Battalions for three hours and caused heavy casualties. The Gordons and Gurkhas were detailed to clear the way. When the Gurkhas faltered, the Gordons' Colonel roared, 'The General says the hill must be taken at all costs. The Gordon Highlanders WILL take it.' With their officers leading and pipers playing, the Gordons charged across the open ground through ferocious fire. They continued up the steep narrow cliff path, still under heavy fire. The enemy tribesmen, incredulous at the Gordons' continued advance, fell back. The Gordons took the Heights of Dargai in just forty minutes. Seven of their men were killed and thirty-seven wounded. Despite the gruelling battle,

THE VICTORIA CROSS AND THE GORDONS

The VC is awarded only for acts of conspicuous gallantry. Instituted by Queen Victoria in 1856 at the end of the Crimean War, the medals are cast from the bronze of guns captured at Sevastopol. No fewer than nineteen Gordon Highlanders have received this highest of all British military awards; eleven of these are proudly displayed in the Gordon Highlanders' Museum in Aberdeen. The first was awarded retrospectively to Private Thomas Beach; although the regiment did not serve in the Crimea, Private Beach was one of several hundred Gordons who fought bravely there, seconded to other units.

The courage of the Gordons at the Heights of Dargai resulted in the award of two VCs to Private Edward Lawson and Piper George Findlater. Piper Findlater, from Forgue in rural Aberdeenshire, is the most famous Gordon Highlander to have been awarded the VC. His citation describes it well: 'during the attack in the Dargai Heights on 20 October 1897, Piper Findlater, after being shot through both feet and unable to stand, sat up under heavy fire and played the regimental march to encourage the charge of the Gordon Highlanders.' The music of the pipes, particularly the Regimental March, 'The Cock o' the North', certainly inspired the Gordons at the Heights of Dargai.

Following action to take the Heights of Dargai,
Gordons carried the wounded down the cliff path;
diorama, The Gordon Highlanders' Museum.
(The Gordon Highlanders' Museum, Aberdeen)

the Gordons then volunteered to carry the wounded Gurkhas and Dorsets' soldiers down the steep rocky track, to the spontaneous cheers of the other regiments. On arrival in Britain, their journey from Liverpool was triumphal. In Edinburgh such huge crowds lined the streets to welcome them that a squadron of Royal Scots Greys was brought in to clear a path for them.

When the Boer War was declared in 1899, the 2nd Battalion of the now-legendary Regiment was already at Ladysmith in South Africa. Later joined by the 1st Battalion, both distinguished themselves in action. Winston Churchill's account of the Battle of Doornkop reflects the importance of the Gordons' role in the victory: 'The honours, equally with the cost of victory, making every allowance for skilful direction and bold leading, belong to the 1st Battalion Gordon Highlanders more than to all the troops put together.' Six VCs were awarded to Gordon Highlanders during the Boer War.

The Gordon Highlanders continued to fight bravely throughout both World Wars and later served in Malaya, Cyprus, Kenya, Swaziland, Borneo, Belize, Northern Ireland, the First Gulf War and with the UN Protection Force in Bosnia. Amalgamated with the Queen's Own Highlanders in 1994, they served as The Highlanders in Kosovo and Iraq. The spirit of the Gordon Highlanders now lives on in 4SCOTS, The Royal Regiment of Scotland, in their dogged determination to 'get the job done' and, not least, in their dry humour even in the face of adversity.

AD 1600–1898

ATTACK OF THE RESURRECTIONISTS!

KING'S COLLEGE, ABERDEEN, had a Chair of Medicine from 1497, the first in the English-speaking world. In 1636 William Gordon, Mediciner at King's College, petitioned for permission to teach anatomy. His request was granted and he was also authorised to receive each year two bodies of rebels or outlaws who had been executed. In the 1700s and early 1800s the demand for corpses for anatomy teaching increased and two per year was no longer sufficient. The only legal source of bodies to meet anatomists' requirements was convicted and executed criminals. As a result, the supply of illegally sourced bodies, supplied by the men known as the Resurrectionists, developed into a lucrative trade.

In the 1700s Aberdeen medical students studied anatomy for a year in Edinburgh. The Aberdeen Medical Society, now the Medico-Chirugical Society, was founded in 1789 by students returning from Edinburgh. Their aim was to ensure anatomy could be studied in Aberdeen. At early Society meetings, the students dissected a dog and also foetuses and still-born children which occasionally 'came their way'. As there were no professional resurrectionists in Aberdeen, Society members had to procure bodies themselves. They were

EARLY GRAVE ROBBERS

In and around Aberdeen not only bodysnatchers took an interest in the contents of graves. One night in the early 1600s, the Sexton at Inverurie opened Merjorie Elphinstone's new grave to take her rings. To his horror, Merjorie awakened from a trance which had been mistaken for death. She quickly recovered and arrived home at midnight, startling her husband and the grieving friends still there. Also in the 1600s, the Beadle of St Machar's Cathedral, Aberdeen, was severely rebuked by the minister for sifting the remains of the dead for their rings and other jewellery. Ghoulish professionals also opened graves to steal jewellery, clothing and teeth which they sold to dentists. Some stripped the corpses of their fat for sale, even to people who knew its origin.

encouraged by former members who were doctors in London and reported that bodies were available there on a daily basis. Meeting minutes refer to members being paid half a guinea if they 'procured a subject' and being fined for shirking bodysnatching duty. One day in the early 1800s, an exhumed body was accidentally left in the Society's Hall. The body was discovered soon afterwards and the students were ordered to rebury it the same evening, monitored by the Town Sergeant. A sympathetic Sheriff fined them one guinea but the fine was never collected.

A 1600s print of head and shoulder dissection. (Thomas Fisher Rare Book Library, University of Toronto)

The rapidly growing trade in bodies for dissection was a serious concern for those recently bereaved and various methods were introduced to outsmart the grave robbers. A large, heavy flat stone known as a 'mortstone' was placed on top of the grave and left there for around six weeks, by which time the body would be too putrefied for dissection. Another protective device was the 'mortsafe'. This extremely heavy iron frame, weighing up to one tonne, was lowered on top of the coffin in its grave. Some had a flat coffin-shaped stone or metal slab attached to the frame, to lie over the coffin. After six weeks mortsafes were dug up, often requiring a block and tackle to do so, stored and reused. Vaults for temporary public use were also built to keep the coffins safe while the body inside decomposed. Called 'morthouses', these were constructed with double doors of wood and iron with strong locks. Some had two locks to allow separate keys to be held by different people. A few were circular and had a turntable inside which was turned each week and the coffins were buried

LIFTING A BODY

The scientific method of resurrecting a corpse was to clear the earth from the head of the coffin and lever up the lid using a special crowbar which was inserted between the body and the wood. The lid usually snapped a third of the way along, allowing the body to be drawn out by rounding the shoulders over the chest and turning it to extract it diagonally. The grave would be reinstated so that only close inspection would reveal any disturbance. Bodies were often concealed in disused buildings until they could be delivered safely. One student ruined his father's bakery business when the corpse he had hidden among bags of flour was discovered.

in order. Kirkyard 'watch-houses' were built, where paid guards or relatives could keep watch nightly until the body was unusable. Vigils were prolonged in winter as colder temperatures preserved the corpse for longer.

Most watch-houses had windows, shot holes and a bell for summoning help if grave robbers appeared. One student, who had exhumed a body at Peterculter and planned to transport it by boat on the River Dee, was thwarted when he was shot in the chest by grave-watchers. Each watch-house had a fireplace, table and chairs. Liquid refreshment, usually alcoholic, was considered essential and inevitably the watchers sometimes fell asleep. In 1829, a woman who had died in childbirth was buried in Aberdeen's Spittal cemetery. Her relatives believed her body would be safe as several watchers were in the graveyard guarding another grave that night. Next morning they found the grave had been disturbed; only the empty coffin and shroud remained. The bodies of the wealthy were rarely stolen as it was easier for bodysnatchers to open the cheaper coffins of the poor. Quiet country graveyards were easy targets as there was less likelihood of witnesses. One student told how he and his brother had driven back from a country kirkyard with the corpse sitting up in the cart between them. Another, desperate for a body to study, found a dead infant on the sea shore. Back at his lodgings, he scandalised his landlady by boiling the corpse in her broth pot to clean the bones.

At Drumoak kirkyard, west of Aberdeen, a body had just been removed when the local blacksmith, a good friend

Skene Mort Safe, now partly hidden by a holly bush – perhaps planted to keep witches away! (Author's collection)

of the deceased, heard of the deed. He immediately stopped shoeing a horse, leapt on its back and gave chase, his face still black from the fire. His approach muffled by the wind, he drew alongside, brandishing his hammer. The students, believing he was Auld Nick, dropped everything and fled.

A lecturer, keen to find the cause of a young boy's death, suggested he be buried in a particular kirkyard so that his students could easily exhume the body. When they attempted to do so, the ground was frozen so hard that the students' spades broke. Undeterred, they broke into the church, took pewter collection ladles to use instead and left them in the kirkyard. Returning to Aberdeen with the body, and with the boy's relatives in hot pursuit, they found their way blocked at the Bridge of Dee by a group of men. The resurrectionist leader, who had the boy's body in a sack, attempted to drop it into a shallow ice hole under the bridge for later retrieval. However, in haste and panic he missed the ice and dropped it

Banchory Cemetery watch house, with the entrance at first-floor level for added security. (Author's collection)

The Anatomy Act of 1832 attempted to end bodysnatching by licensing anatomists and making provision for their legal access to bodies unclaimed forty-eight hours after death. In Aberdeen, however, the desecration of graves continued, at least in one cemetery. In 1898 William Coutts, superintendent of Nellfield Cemetery, was committed for trial when it was discovered he habitually lifted bones and bodies of both adults and children, broke them if necessary, and reburied them under paths and in other parts of the cemetery. It is thought he did this to make space for new burials and to avoid the effort of digging fresh graves. Coffins, and possibly also their contents, were burned in the cemetery's furnace.

into the water, from where it was rescued by the boy's relatives.

Aberdeen anatomist Andrew Moir did not insist on careful reburial of dissected remains. One day in 1831, a dog unearthed a mangled human limb behind his anatomy theatre, watched closely by some children. The news spread rapidly and a furious mob gathered and broke into the theatre. They ejected Moir and his students, who fled before the mob found the three bodies laid out for dissection. The mob recovered the bodies, smashed the building and set it on fire. Troops called from the local barracks just stood and watched while the building burned.

Watch house at Banchory-Devenick Kirkyard, with solid metal mort safe in the foreground. (Author's collection)

SHIPWRECK!

ABERDEEN HAS BEEN an established port for around 900 years. Protected by the rocky cliffs of Girdleness to the south and the large sandy promontory of Sandness to the north, the River Dee estuary formed a natural anchorage. Vessels would anchor in the Gawpuyl, the part of the harbour now called the Turning Basin. Smaller craft would head out to them with new cargoes and provisions and to bring back the discharged cargo. The city's links with the sea run deep, and trading, fishing, shipbuilding, whaling and passengers have all brought prosperity. Aberdeen's patron saint is St Nicholas, also patron saint of sailors. Over the centuries, Aberdonians have manned lifeboats and carried out shore rescues. Shipwrecks have had a profound effect on the city and its people.

Aberdeen Shipmasters Society was founded in 1598 to look after distressed sailors and their families. As the approach to the port was extremely hazardous, the society also put pressure on the town council and magistrates to improve navigation. Shortly before he became King James I of England, James VI granted the society a Charter and made provision for funds to be raised for harbour improvements. In 1607 a bulwark was built on the south side which helped deepen the entrance.

Following the Act of Union of 1707, trade increased dramatically and

ST FITTICK'S CHURCH

It is said that one person to be shipwrecked at the end of the 1100s was a Frenchman who was washed ashore uninjured. In gratitude for his survival, he had a church built nearby dedicated to St Fiacre, now known locally as St Fittick. The ruins of the church, which can be seen today, date from 1242 and overlook the Bay of Nigg to the south of Girdleness. As was customary then, the church was built with a leper window, so that the many people who suffered from leprosy in the north of Scotland at that time could watch the service through the window without infecting people in the church.

Wreck of the whaler Oscar, *1 April 1813, by Alexander G. Spark. (© Aberdeen Art Gallery & Museums Collections)*

the port was developed throughout the 1700s and early 1800s. A major development was the North Pier, built in stages to provide shelter from easterly winds and a barrier to sand and shingle drifting south from the beach. It also enhanced the natural scour of the river.

By the early 1800s, Aberdeen was an important whaling port. Each spring, whaling ships would set sail for the Arctic. Most carried a crew of around fifty which included the master, mate, surgeon, harpooners, seamen and, for each of the small whale-chaser boats, a steersman, harpoon linesman, landsman and apprentice.

The 1 April 1813 dawned clear and calm as five whalers prepared to depart for the Greenland whaling grounds. While at anchor in Aberdeen Bay, a violent snowstorm suddenly blew in, with the gale increasing quickly to

hurricane force. Even the strongest crewmen had difficulty keeping their feet. Three whalers returned to port, another weighed anchor to ride out the storm, leaving the fifth, the *Oscar*, in the bay. There she waited too long at anchor for her boat to bring the last of her crew. When she did weigh anchor, she was too close to shore and, with no room to manoeuvre, she was driven onto the rocks of Greyhope Bay. The large crowd which quickly gathered nearby included relatives of the crew and seafarers who understood only too well the power of the sea and wind. However, the *Oscar's* position on the rocks meant that no one could approach, either on foot or by boat. Her crew cut down the main mast in an attempt to make a bridge to the nearest rocks, but the mast fell the wrong way. Men clinging to the rigging were knocked off when the fore and mizzen masts fell. Those who had come to help could only stand and watch in horror as sailors were washed into the sea by huge waves and the few who almost made it ashore were swept away like their crewmates. Of the forty-four-man crew, forty-two were drowned that day. The sole survivors were seaman James Venus and first mate John Jameson, who was miraculously rescued by his uncle. Captain Richard Jameson was among the crowd of would-be rescuers when he spotted something floating in the surf. Snagging it and pulling it ashore with his long staff, he was surprised and delighted to discover it was his nephew.

The bodies were laid out for identification on the steps of the Sugar House, on what is now Regent Quay, and most were later buried together in a common grave in St Fittick's kirkyard. Their legacy is Girdleness Lighthouse, built twenty years later following huge public support for a warning beacon. Designed by the renowned civil engineer Robert Stevenson, it originally had one light in the top dome and another lower down within a glazed gallery to differentiate it from other lighthouses on the north east coast. The lower light was removed in 1890 when a clockwork turntable was installed allowing the upper light to flash. Today, its 'character' is two flashes of white light every twenty seconds. It is also one of only three lighthouses in Scotland to provide Differential Global Positioning System transmissions.

Exactly forty years to the day after the *Oscar* tragedy, the passenger paddle steamer *Duke of Sutherland* was also wrecked at the very entrance to Aberdeen Harbour. Travel by steamer was popular at the time and the *Duke of Sutherland* was carrying a full cargo and twenty-five passengers from London. As she approached the harbour entrance a sudden south-easterly storm blew up. Combined with the powerful currents of the River Dee in spate and a strong flood tide, the squall forced the vessel off course and onto the North Pier, smashing her hull. With seawater pouring in, her furnaces were engulfed and power to the paddles was lost. Nothing could be done to regain control and the vessel began to break up. The ship's lifeboat was lowered and took eight people on board before being driven off by the wind. The harbour lifeboat rescued another fifteen before it was itself damaged. A salmon coble, manned by six volunteers, capsized on the way to the wreck and five of the crew were drowned. Attempts were made to fire the rocket and lifelines stored in the Roundhouse on Pocra Quay but this was hindered by lack of experience and damp gunpowder. The captain was washed into the sea and lost, leaving the chief steward to take charge of the rescue of a further twenty people by lifeline from the ship to the pier. He was later recognised for his bravery. A total of sixteen people died that day. The public were outraged and demanded answers – how could people drown so close to land and safety, with rescue equipment nearby? The poor condition of the lifeboat and lack of training in the use of lifeline rockets were implicated. Questions were asked in Parliament as to how it could be ensured that equipment already in place could be used more efficiently.

The River Dee changed its course naturally several times until in 1868 the river was deliberately diverted into the artificial channel where it still flows today. At the time, Aberdeen Corporation also intended to build a bridge across the channel to replace the ferryboats which linked Torry with the city. However, no bridge was built at that time.

The 5 April 1876 was a holiday, with a traditional fair taking place in Torry and long queues of people waiting to travel to and fro. The ferryboat was operated by pulley and hawser and was approved for thirty-two seated passengers. Typically for the time, as many standing passengers as possible were crammed aboard, with children tucked into every available space. With seventy on board, the ferry was certainly overloaded and panic broke out when it was caught by the current of the river in spate combined with the strong flood tide. It started to take water. In a vain attempt to avert disaster the hawser was cut but the boat still capsized, spilling everyone into the icy swirling waters of the River Dee. That day thirty-two people, including several children, were swept away and drowned. They too left a legacy, as only

After some delay, Captain Manby's apparatus was used to rescue survivors from the Duke of Sutherland. *(© Aberdeen Art Gallery & Museums Collections)*

five years later the long-planned bridge was opened. Named for Queen Victoria, it was paid for not only by Aberdeen Corporation but also by outraged citizens who contributed towards its cost.

AD 1914–1918

THE WAR TO END ALL WARS

THE FIRST WORLD War was to be the war to end all wars. It was fought at sea and, for the first time, in the air. On land it was artillery and infantry warfare on a massive scale. Around 10 million military personnel of all nationalities died or were reported missing. In France and Flanders alone over 380,000 British Army soldiers were killed, a further 145,000 were listed missing and 175,000 taken prisoner. Almost 2 million suffered appalling injuries, including poison gas inhalation and limbs shattered by shell fire. Amputation was commonplace either immediately or shortly after injury because of infection, mostly tetanus or gas gangrene. Around 150,000 died of their wounds. The Battle of the Somme in 1916 claimed 432,000 British casualties; 150,000 of these were killed in action or died from their wounds. Another 100,000 were so seriously injured they could no longer serve in any capacity. On the first day of that battle alone, almost 20,000 were killed – most before 9 a.m. These young men became Britain's 'lost generation'. For the first time, women had a role to play. Many filled professional and other positions left vacant by the men fighting abroad. Some volunteered for the Scottish Women's Hospitals. One cycled from Angus, south of Aberdeen, to Flanders to do so.

The reasons for this war were complex, perhaps fully understood only by the politicians of the day. The catalyst was the assassination in Sarajevo on 28 June 1914 of Archduke Franz Ferdinand. On Sunday, 2 August, the congregation in the Kirk of St Nicholas, Aberdeen, was told war was inevitable. At 7 p.m. the following day, Britain declared war on Germany.

A massive civilian army was mobilised. A small part of this was the U (University) Company, a Territorial unit of the Gordon Highlanders. It was unique, comprising students, graduates and teaching staff of Aberdeen University. Its sergeants and colour sergeants were promoted for one year only to allow others also to experience leadership. Mobilised to go to war in November 1914, this was arguably the most intelligent and best-educated unit in the British Army. Their first taste of real army life was in Bedford as part of the 51st Highland Division. They grumbled about irrelevant inspections and petty discipline and were concerned about lack of equipment, appropriate clothing and footwear.

The front line comprised separate positions 15 metres apart, each with a few men. As these reminded the Gordons of shooting hides on Aberdeenshire's grouse moors, they named them the Grouse Butts. No movement was permitted during the day. Lights and fires were banned after dark. Troop movements, although always carried out under cover of darkness, were extremely dangerous. The men, up to their knees in mud and occasionally falling into man-deep, water-filled shell holes, had to carry water, food and ammunition to the front line. Should a star shell burst, illuminating the area, they had to freeze instantly in the hope they would be mistaken for brushwood.

As part of the 4th Battalion, U Company left for France in February 1915. The regular battalions had already suffered devastating losses; one Gordons' unit had lost sixteen of their eighteen pipers within two weeks of arrival. The enemy had been preparing for war for many years and was well equipped with heavy artillery and shells, while 4th Gordons lacked sufficient ammunition. By the end of the month, U Company was in Belgium, very close to the British artillery, with one gun just 200 metres away.

By 4 March, U Company was under fire. Dressed in kilts and greatcoats, armed with their rifles and thirty rounds of ammunition, they carried sandbags, picks and shovels and marched 4 miles through 'oceans of mud'. With 'bullets tearing overhead', they dug 'rests' in a trench to fill their sandbags and to drain water from the trench. Soon they were on the front line. The Germans fired star shells during the night to prevent attack. At dawn, heavy artillery fire started. Falling shrapnel raised huge clouds of earth. Each time the sandbag parapet was blown in, the men could not rebuild it until after dark, so had to crouch in the shallow trench, often for several hours. The German snipers were accurate. One sergeant 'had his brains blown out by an explosive bullet. His cap went about 8 feet in the air.' Listening post duty required the man to lie on the ground in front of the trench, with bullets flying just 2ft above. After six days on the front line the men faced further exhaustion with a full day's march to the relative safety of the billets for four days. By the end of August, most of the men of U Company had been wounded at least once.

From the safety of their position over 30 miles behind the front line, High Command planned an offensive at Loos in Northern France together with several small, diversionary battles. One of these was to be at Hooge, near

Trench at Festubert, Artois, 1915. (The Gordon Highlanders' Museum, Aberdeen)

Ypres in Belgium, and 4th Gordons trained intensively for ten days for this diversionary attack. Their training camp, surrounded by fields of red poppies, was plagued with flies and mosquitoes and many suffered from dysentery. When they arrived at Hooge the planned attack was far from being a secret. Even the Germans were aware and displayed placards on their barbed wire, 'Why not attack today, Jocks? Why wait until the 25th?' Three days before the action, Field Marshal Lord Kitchener addressed 4th Gordons, making it clear their action was a sacrifice to assist the main offensive at Loos. He wished them 'as much luck as they could expect'.

Just after 4 a.m. on 25 September 1915, following artillery bombardment of German lines, the 4th Gordons, flanked by 1st Gordons and 2nd Royal Scots, went 'over the top' into heavy rain. The artillery fire had failed to create many gaps in the German barbed-wire defences. The wire ahead of U Company had been breached but the 1st Gordons ran into uncut wire and deadly machine-gun fire. The few

Colonel Alistair Gordon, 1st Battalion Gordon Highlanders, wounded and waiting for dark to be evacuated for medical treatment. (The Gordon Highlanders' Museum, Aberdeen)

men left standing joined U Company to attack three lines of German trenches and successfully take their objective, a field gun. However, under heavy bombardment, they were forced to withdraw. With only a few bombs and wet emery paper with which to ignite them, U Company was forced back to its previous position. Of the three Battalions which launched the offensive, only a few men remained.

Following this 'small battle', thirty-two officers and 635 other ranks of the 1st and 4th Gordons were listed as killed,

THE GORDONS' LIFE IN THE FLANDERS TRENCHES

With little natural cover, the armies dug trenches for basic protection. In dry soil, deep zigzag trenches could be dug relatively easily. In Flanders the water table is particularly high; after the wet winter, digging deep trenches was impossible. Often less than a metre deep, sandbags were used to increase their height but these did not always stop bullets and shrapnel. The sticky mud in the waterlogged trenches sucked off socks, shoes and spats and sometimes even kilts. Sandbags on their bare feet were the only protection from frostbite. When finally issued with thigh-high, sheepskin-lined gumboots they were horrified to discover there were only two pairs per platoon of thirty men. It was impossible to dig latrines because of the water. The men became infested with body lice which gathered in the seams of their shirts and the pleats of their kilts.

Above *Gordon Highlanders in their trench at Neuve Chapelle. (The Gordon Highlanders' Museum, Aberdeen)*

Left *A working party, filling sandbags, similar to work U Company did. (The Gordon Highlanders' Museum, Aberdeen)*

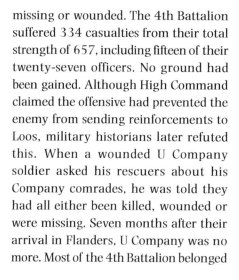

missing or wounded. The 4th Battalion suffered 334 casualties from their total strength of 657, including fifteen of their twenty-seven officers. No ground had been gained. Although High Command claimed the offensive had prevented the enemy from sending reinforcements to Loos, military historians later refuted this. When a wounded U Company soldier asked his rescuers about his Company comrades, he was told they had all either been killed, wounded or were missing. Seven months after their arrival in Flanders, U Company was no more. Most of the 4th Battalion belonged

to Aberdeen and adjoining parts of Aberdeenshire. In the city everyone was either directly affected or had close friends, relatives or neighbours who had lost their young men.

This war, which did not end all wars, had a huge and long-lasting impact on the lives of the people of Aberdeen, Scotland and the whole of Britain. Those who died at Hooge, just one 'small battle', were only a few of the 100,000 who died serving in Scotland's ten infantry regiments and a tiny fraction of the 659,000 men lost by Britain in this war. The lives of a whole generation were ruined. Men were killed or maimed and many survivors were left with minds shattered by shell shock. Women were denied marriage and motherhood. They became Britain's 'spinster generation'.

AD 1939–1945

WAR IN THE STREETS OF ABERDEEN

IN 1939, BRITAIN was again at war. This time the objective was clear – to stop the spread of fascism and to prevent Nazi invasion. In Aberdeen, as elsewhere in Britain, the war was not only fought far away on land and sea but also in the skies above. Enemy aircraft brought this war into the streets, killing and wounding civilians, destroying their homes and disrupting their lives as never before.

When Britain declared war on Germany on 3 September 1939, 2nd Battalion Gordon Highlanders were on garrison duty in Singapore. The 1st Gordons were in Aldershot but very soon had crossed the Channel with three battalions of Gordons' Territorials to fight in France and Flanders. Many Aberdonians were already serving in the Royal Navy or aboard merchant ships. At RAF Dyce, now Aberdeen International Airport, 612 Squadron was at that time flying coastal patrols. Later, reconnaissance aircraft and fighters were based there.

In France, two Gordons' Battalions had been evacuated from Dunkirk in early June 1941. However, the 1st and 5th Gordons (part of the 51st Highland Division), faced with the overwhelming might of the

Wehrmacht and with no hope of rescue by sea, surrendered at St Valéry. They spent the remainder of the war as prisoners. Following the bombing of Pearl Harbor by the Japanese in December 1941, the USA entered the war. The Japanese moved relentlessly south through Malaya and, despite stiff resistance by Allied troops including 2nd Gordons, Singapore fell on 15 February 1942. The surviving Gordons spent the rest of the war in appalling conditions as prisoners of the Japanese, starved and forced to work as slaves on the Burma Railway.

Despite worrying about their loved ones in far-flung places and grieving for those who had died, for many Aberdonians the war must have seemed remote. This changed when in April 1940 the Nazis invaded Norway, just one hour's flying time from Aberdeen. Following the invasion of Norway, Aberdeen endured many bombing raids and suffered more raids than any other Scottish town or city. On 372 occasions the sirens screamed their air-raid warnings. Sometimes the 'all clear' would sound within a few minutes as the aircraft only passed overhead while heading to other targets. However, from 26 June 1940 to

21 April 1943, Aberdeen was itself the target of thirty-four separate attacks. A total of 178 civilians were killed, ninety-seven of these in a single night. Railway lines, engineering works, factories and, in particular, the shipyards and harbour were prime targets. In the first few raids, all during darkness, incendiary and high-explosive bombs fell mostly on Torry as the Luftwaffe pilots tried to hit the harbour and shipyards. On 12 July they returned in daylight with no warning of their approach. Around sixteen high-explosive bombs hit the Hall Russell shipyard, most falling on the boiler house, killing thirty-two people and injuring around thirty more. One young shipyard worker survived only because he was thrown into the water. Fortunately, Royal Navy ships under construction and repair were not damaged. High-explosive bombs also fell near Kings College, on Castlehill Barracks, around Urquhart Road and on the railway line nearby. Not all exploded. One of the aircraft, a Heinkel bomber, was shot down by the RAF and crashed onto the Ice Rink near the southern end of Aberdeen's ring road, Anderson Drive.

The Heinkel bomber shot down by the RAF crashed on the Ice Rink, Aberdeen, 12 July 1940. (Aberdeen City and Aberdeenshire Archives)

The raids continued throughout 1940 and 1941. The Aberdeen coast was the first landfall for Nazi planes. Unless spotted by patrolling aircraft or ships, bombers could be overhead before any warning was sounded. Aircraft, damaged by anti-aircraft fire and forced to turn back before reaching their main target, such as Clydebank or Greenock, would drop their bombs to lighten the load before crossing the North Sea. Aberdeen, Peterhead and Fraserburgh were useful secondary targets. At night, despite strict blackout, Aberdeen's silver granite buildings shone in starlight and provided easy targets on moonlit nights; at that time buildings in many other British cities were blackened by soot. Some raids, by just one aircraft, were called 'tip-and-run'. Others were more sustained. Attacks on RAF Dyce fortunately caused little damage. A decoy airport, complete with false runway lights, was set up in the countryside nearby. Early in 1941 the Muchalls railway viaduct, just south of Aberdeen, was hit but not badly damaged. However, the aircrew raked a nearby passenger train with gunfire. Planes also strafed the city with machine-gun fire. A father and his young son were shot while working in their garden. Bombs frequently fell on residential areas close to engineering works, factories and the harbour. Injury or death was a huge risk for those caught at home, unable or unwilling to go to the air-raid shelters in time.

After victory in the Battle of Britain, autumn and winter 1942–43 brought temporary respite for Aberdonians and in April some of the city's anti-aircraft guns were sent south to reinforce

ABERDEEN AND THE NORWEGIAN RESISTANCE

Aberdeen's proximity to Norway was of vital importance to the Special Operations Executive. Norwegian refugees, mostly young single men wanting to fight for their country, travelled to Scotland in appalling weather and under cover of the long winter nights, mostly in fishing boats and occasionally in open boats. Many left their friends in Norway with the wish, 'See you in Aberdeen!' They usually arrived in Shetland and occasionally on the east coast of Scotland. Many of the men joined the Free Norwegian forces. Others were recruited for the Norwegian resistance and were trained at Glenmore in the Cairngorm Mountains, west of Aberdeen, where the terrain is similar to parts of Norway. The Norwegian fishing boats were based in Shetland and made the dangerous voyage many times as they delivered radios, explosives, arms and resistance fighters to take part in daring raids in occupied Norway in an operation known as The Shetland Bus. They frequently returned with additional refugees as well as resistance fighters. The whole operation was co-ordinated from Aberdeen, strategically placed between Shetland and the Cairngorms. Its enthusiastic liaison officer was Captain John Cowie, a Gordon Highlander who worked tirelessly to ensure the success of the whole operation.

Captain John Cowie, Gordon Highlanders, liaison officer for Norwegian Resistance activities. (Reproduced with kind permission of Capt Cowie's daughter, Mrs Isabell Jack)

defences there. However, following the sustained bombing of Berlin and its citizens by RAF and Russian aircraft, Hitler ordered revenge on Britain's cities. On the night of 21 April 1943, Aberdeen was the first to be bombed. One of the best Luftwaffe squadrons had been brought to Sola-Stavanger airbase in south west Norway. Each Dornier 217 bomber was refuelled, armed and loaded with three tonnes of high-explosive bombs. They crossed the North Sea in little more than half an hour. With no warning, the first wave of ten aircraft came in low at intervals of around a minute. The second wave of fifteen flew in at 6,000ft. The bombs fell mostly in residential areas, creating terror and killing civilians. In just forty-five minutes, over 130 high-explosive, cluster and incendiary bombs fell on Aberdeen, leaving whole streets ablaze and killing entire families. Children had been playing in the streets. Some were strafed by the enemy aircraft as they walked home from a Boys' Brigade display at the city's Music Hall. One boy's foot caught fire when he stepped

Above *Homes ruined in Stafford Street, Aberdeen, by the blitz of 21 April 1943. (Aberdeen City and Aberdeenshire Archives)*

Right *In the aftermath of the April 1943 bombing raid, damaged houses were repaired in the most practical way possible – these houses still have flat roofs today. (Author's collection)*

in phosphorus. That night in Aberdeen ninety-seven civilians and twenty-seven soldiers died and 235 were wounded, including ninety-three seriously. Around 9,000 homes were badly damaged, 600 of them no longer habitable. Schools, churches, railway lines, the mental hospital, a textile factory, cemetery, barracks and electricity substations were also hit. Although war-weary Aberdonians did not know it, this was the city's, and Scotland's, last air raid.

As Aberdonians reeled in shock from the blitz, Britain and her allies were at last beginning to win the fight. In October 1942 the reformed 51st Highland Division, including 1st and 5th/7th Gordons, spearheaded the fight back at El Alamein in Egypt, driving the enemy to retreat across North Africa to Tunis. In the spring of 1943, 6th Gordons joined the fighting in Tunisia and by May the war in North Africa was

over. As the war started to turn in favour of the Allies, an interesting aircraft landed at RAF Dyce. It was a German Junkers 88 night fighter, fitted with the latest radar, whose crew wanted to defect. Both aircraft and crew were of great value to the intelligence services. In July 1943, 1st and 5th/7th Gordons fought in the invasion of Sicily. At the end of the year, 6th Gordons arrived in Italy and fought steadily north. Meantime, 1st and 5th/7th Gordons had been recalled to the UK to train for D-Day. They landed in Normandy in June 1944 and, joined by 2nd Gordons, fought their way across Europe and into Germany, playing a vital role in the liberation of Europe. Norway was liberated from its five-year Nazi occupation and victory in Europe was celebrated on 8 May 1945. In Burma, however, Gordons were still fighting with the Royal Artillery and Royal Armoured Corps against the Japanese. On 15 August 1945, the war in the Far East was finally over. The Gordon Highlanders had been among the first soldiers to fight in 1939 and were among the last to be stood down in 1945. In Aberdeen, bonfires were lit in celebration of peace.

CODA

The Real Price of North Sea Oil and Gas

MOST PEOPLE THINK about the price of oil and gas only when they complain about the cost of filling their car or paying for their central heating. Few consider the real cost of the UK's oil and gas: the price paid by so many North Sea workers and their families in life-changing injuries, both physical and mental, and the lives lost in the battle to discover and produce the oil and gas which lie trapped between layers of rock deep below the North Sea.

Around 25,000 people work on 275 oil and gas installations in the North Sea. Others work aboard the specialist vessels which support these platforms and drilling rigs. Many offshore workers live in and around Aberdeen, the offshore industry's main hub. Very few of the offshore workforce are female, although more and more shore-based professional posts are being filled by women. This is also a relatively young industry, still learning from its mistakes. Huge investment is required to find and bring the oil and gas ashore and there is often massive pressure to avoid delays and to complete work on schedule, even if this increases the risks. The commute to work is like no other. Each year around half a million workers leave Aberdeen International Airport's four helicopter terminals on helicopter 'commuter flights' – this is almost certainly the world's busiest heliport.

Travelling offshore by helicopter is very different from flying in a commercial aircraft. Passengers must wear a lifejacket and survival suit with at least three layers underneath – some are also required to wear a onesie beneath that, all to help survive the low water temperature should the helicopter have to ditch in the sea. The cockpit can be a hot and humid workplace, so flight crew may, under certain clearly defined circumstances, be allowed to wear cotton flying suits – their concentration takes top priority. All travelling have offshore safety certification including experience in the Helicopter Underwater Escape Trainer, which simulates controlled and uncontrolled ditching on water. Pilots' training also focuses on managing the aftermath of any ditching, their priorities being getting everyone on board the inflatable liferafts, treating life-threatening injuries and administering very necessary sea-sickness medication.

People may not be well-adapted to the hostile environment of the North Sea but the helicopters are. These are

MAN-RIDING

This is a fairly common offshore operation. A man is suspended in a sling and lowered by winch to carry out work in places where scaffolding is not practical.

One autumn evening in 2000, a man-riding job went horribly wrong on a drilling rig 120 miles east of Aberdeen. An assistant derrickman was lowered by winch to carry out work between the Drill Floor above him and the Blow Out Preventer deck below. The winch and winchman were well out of sight above the Drill Floor, with the winch-line passing through a small hole. This, the 'mousehole', is around 25cm in diameter on top, widening underneath to an oval about 30 by 45cm. With the work completed, the winchman was given the order to raise the sling. When the order came to stop, the winch kept rising – the winchman had not heard, despite frantic shouts, radio and tannoy calls. The winch pulled the sling and the man inexorably upwards into the mousehole, causing fatal injuries.

modern, high-spec aircraft, built to the operators' specific requirements. Their pilots must be good systems managers, problem solvers and team players able to 'think out of the box'. In the early days of the industry most pilots were ex-military but now more come through civilian training programmes. A few are women. All are passionate pilots.

Depending on helicopter type and installation location, the journey will last from thirty to ninety minutes. It will be noisy, smelly and uncomfortable with no noise-insulation, no aircon, no toilet and no cabin attendants. With up to nineteen passengers, mostly large muscular men, dressed in multiple layers and life jackets, it is also extremely cramped. The only movie is the mandatory pre-boarding safety briefing film. Both passengers and baggage are weighed to allow detailed fuel calculation and the flight plan must include an onshore diversion point. Thunder clouds, wind direction and speed, turbulence, a technical problem or offshore emergency may

prevent the helicopter landing on its destination installation, so the pilots must be prepared to make a planned landing either back in Scotland or in Norway. Rotating helicopter blades generate a charge; this could trigger a lightning strike, which could take out the electronic equipment or puncture a rotor blade. Cloud, visibility, ice, sea and wind conditions must be within prescribed limits. The highest wind speed allowed for operation is 60 knots, Violent Storm Force 11, when it is difficult for a man to keep his feet and wave heights are likely to be 11.5–16 metres. Wind above 64 knots is classed as a hurricane force. Rescue from wave heights over 10 metres is extremely hazardous. Understandably, some offshore workers are frightened, even terrified, of flying by helicopter. Company mentoring programmes help a few; others give up their jobs rather than endure their nightmare commute.

Helicopters are also required for medivac flights, transporting injured or ill workers to Aberdeen Royal Infirmary or farther afield for specialist treatment. Divers in saturation are taken to the National Hyperbaric Centre in Aberdeen in decompression chambers. In 2012, two divers working from the Diving Support Vessel *Bibby Topaz* were fortunate to survive when the ship's dynamic positioning failed and she drifted off course, snagging the divers' umbilicals, the hoses which deliver breathing gases and hot water to maintain body temperature. One umbilical was severed, cutting the diver off from all his support systems and he was unconscious by the time the ship got back on course and found him, over thirty minutes later. Cared for by their colleagues in a decompression chamber, both divers had recovered by the time the ship arrived back in Aberdeen some days later.

Throughout the night of 6 July 1988, the sound of constant helicopter traffic alerted Aberdonians to the world's worst offshore oil disaster as the injured were flown to Aberdeen Royal Infirmary. It had been a day much like any other on board the Piper Alpha Platform, 120 miles north east of Aberdeen. Routine maintenance was being carried out on a pressure safety valve from one of the two pumps which controlled the flow of gas to the mainland from Piper and several other fields. Instructions were left by the day shift that this pump must not be used, but were not relayed to the night shift. During the evening, when the second pump failed, the disabled pump was switched on. Gas escaped and almost immediately ignited, causing a huge explosion. Safety-Standby vessels *Sandhaven* and *Silver Pit* launched their fast rescue craft and the specialist fire-fighting vessel *Tharos* sprayed the burning platform with water, but all were driven back when the high pressure pipelines from the other fields also exploded. Helicopters were beaten back by the dense black smoke and soaring flames. On board the burning platform, workers trying to reach the lifeboats were defeated by the flames. Although warned they were leaping to certain death, some still jumped into the sea to escape the blistering flames and toxic fumes. Thirty metres below, the surface of the sea was ablaze with burning oil. Just three hours after the disabled pump was turned on, Piper Alpha collapsed with many men trapped inside.

Of the 226 men on board, 165 died, in addition to two crewmen from *Sandhaven*. Of the sixty-one survivors, thirty-seven were rescued by *Silver Pit*. Seven George Medals were awarded to crewmen of the *Silver Pit* and *Sandhaven* for their acts of great bravery that night; one is on display in Aberdeen Maritime Museum. One survivor said, 'It was only when we stepped outside, then we saw the enormity of the situation. It was your worst nightmare come true. This was Hell … The metal was melting, it was like a surrealist painting, like Dalí's watch.'

The tragedy touched everyone living and working in and around Aberdeen. That morning, traffic moved slowly on the main commuter routes into the city 'almost as though no one wanted to arrive and find out it was true', according to one driver. The long enquiry which followed resulted in over 100 practical recommendations for improved offshore health and safety practices. Piper Alpha's legacy was a changed working culture. The industry learned from its mistakes and continues to learn.

DEDICATED TO
THE MEMORY OF THE
ONE HUNDRED AND SIXTY SEVEN MEN
WHO LOST THEIR LIVES
IN THE
PIPER ALPHA OIL PLATFORM DISASTER

6TH JULY 1988

The Piper Alpha Memorial commemorates the 167 men who died on 6 July 1988. It is in the North Sea Memorial Garden, Hazlehead Park, Aberdeen. (Author's collection)

Sadly, avoidable accidents continue to happen offshore, particularly when there is pressure to complete a job quickly. Even twenty-five years after Piper Alpha, the culture of 'workers do, managers think' still exists in some companies and on some installations. In that twenty-five years, a further 111 men and one woman have lost their lives offshore, around half in helicopter crashes.

SOURCES AND REFERENCES

Books

Adie, George, *Our Air-raid Shelter at 16–18 Cranford Terrace* (Aberdeen, ANESFHS)

Cameron, Alison S. and Stones, Judith A., *Aberdeen an in-depth view of the city's past* (Edinburgh, Society of Antiquaries of Scotland)

Cluer, Andrew, *Walkin' the Mat* (Aberdeen, Lantern Books)

Coventry, Martin, *Castles of the Clans* (Musselburgh, Goblinshead)

Black Kalendar of Aberdeen (Aberdeen, James Strachan)

Davidson, Revd John, *Inverurie and the Earldom of The Garioch* (Aberdeen, A. Brown & Co.)

Ferguson, K., *Black Kalendar of Aberdeen 1746–1878 index* (Aberdeen, ANESFHS)

Henderson, Diana M., *Scotland's Regiments* (Glasgow, Harper Collins)

Howarth, David, *The Shetland Bus* (Lerwick, The Shetland Times Ltd)

Huntly, Marquess of, *The Cock o' the North* (London, Thornton Butterworth Ltd)

Iversen, Kaare, *Shetland Bus Man* (Lerwick, The Shetland Times Ltd)

Keith, Alexander, *A Thousand Years of Aberdeen* (Aberdeen, Aberdeen University Press)

Leslie, Colonel K.H. of Balquhain, *Historical Records of the Family of Leslie 1067–1868-9*

McConachie, John, *The Student Soldiers* (Elgin, Moravian Press Ltd)

MacDonald, Lyn, *The Roses of No Man's Land* (London, Penguin Books)

McKean, Charles, *Banff and Buchan: An Illustrated Architectural Guide* (Edinburgh, RIAS)

McNeill, F. Marian, *The Silver Bough Vol. 1: Scottish Folklore and Folk-Belief* (Glasgow, William Maclellan)

Mcpherson, J. M., *Primitive Beliefs in the Northeast of Scotland* (London, Longmans, Green & Co, 1929)

Marren, Peter, *Grampian Battlefields* (Aberdeen, Aberdeen University Press)

Marshall, Rosalind K., *Queen of Scots* (Edinburgh, HMSO)

Mitchell, G.A.G., *The Book of Aberdeen; Resurrection Days* (Aberdeen 1939, ed. David Rorie)

Morgan, Diane, *The Villages of Aberdeen: Footdee* (Aberdeen, Denburn Books)

Ralston, Ian & Inglis, Jim, *Foul Hordes – The Picts in the North East and their Background* (Aberdeen, University of Aberdeen Anthropological Museum)

Ritchie, Anna, *Picts* (Historic Scotland)

Ritchie, Graham and Anna, *SCOTLAND Archaeology and Early History* (Edinburgh, Edinburgh University Press)

Rodger, E.H.B., *Aberdeen Doctors; Resurrection Days* (Blackwood & Co. Edinburgh and London, 1893)

Ross, Stewart, *Monarchs of Scotland* (Moffat, Lochar Publishing)

Scott, Patrick W., *History of Strathbogie* (Tiverton, XL Publishing Services)

Shepherd, Ian, *Aberdeenshire, Donside and Strathbogie: An illustrated architectural guide* (Edinburgh, RIAS)

Shepherd, Ian, *Exploring Scotland's Heritage: Aberdeen and North-East Scotland* (HMSO)

Shepherd, Ian A.G. and Ralston, Ian B.M., *Early Grampian* (Aberdeen, Grampian Regional Council)

Skelton, Douglas, *Indian Peter* (Edinburgh, Mainstream Publishing)

Smith, Alexander, *A New History of Aberdeenshire* (Aberdeen, Lewis Smith)

Steele, Tom *Scotland's Story* (London, Fontana/Collins)

Sturlason, Snorre, Laing, S. (trans) and Monsen, E.(ed), *Heimskringla (The Lives of the Norse Kings)*

Sutherland, Elizabeth, *The Pictish Guide* (Edinburgh, Birlinn Limited)

Tabraham, Christopher (ed.), *Scotland BC* (Edinburgh, HMSO)

Urquhart, Alistair, *The Forgotten Highlander* (London, Little, Brown)

Wyness, Fenton, *City by the Grey North Sea* (Aberdeen, Impulse Books)

BOOKLETS, GUIDEBOOKS AND SIMILAR

Allen, Grieg Dawson, *The Pursuit of Witches* (Aberdeen, Leopard Magazine, October 2002)

A Guide to Dunnottar Castle (Dunecht, Dunecht Estates)

BBC *History* magazine (Vol. 12, no. 1)

Corgarff Castle Official Souvenir Guide (Historic Scotland)

Croly, Christopher P., *Aberdeen's Castle* (Aberdeen City Council)

Croly, Christopher P., *The Battle of Harlaw* (Aberdeen City Council)

Croly, Christopher P. *Aberdeen's Jacobite Trail* (Aberdeen City Council)

Edinburgh Castle Official Souvenir Guide (Historic Scotland)

Huntly Castle Official Souvenir Guide (Historic Scotland)

Jillings, K.J. *Plague, Pox and the physician in Aberdeen, 1495–1516* (Edinburgh, Royal College of Physicians, 2010)

Kildrummy Castle Official Souvenir Guide (Historic Scotland)

Lonach Gathering and Games 1993 (programme)

Report on the wreck of the Oscar (Aberdeen Journal, 7 April 1813)

Reports on the Aberdeen Blitz (Aberdeen Press and Journal, April 2013)

Statistical Account of Scotland 1791–99: Vol. 19, City of Aberdeen: Vol. 6. Kinneff (Edinburgh)

Vallar, Cindy, *Scottish Pirates*

Wizard Laird's dance with the Devil (Edinburgh, The Scotsman, 2006)

Woolfson, Dr Charles, *Death of an Offshore Worker,* (Aberdeen, Oilc)

ONLINE

www.aberdeencity.co.uk Witches and Witchcraft in Aberdeen

www.bbc.co.uk First World War Casualties

www.educationscotland.gov.uk Scotland's History

www.gordonhighlanders.co.uk

www.historylearningsite.co.uk World War Two

www.raf.mod.uk Battle of Britain campaign diaries and World War Two air stations

www.royal.gov.uk The Crown Jewels; the Honours of Scotland

www.thegordonhighlanders.co.uk

www.theroyalscotsgrenadiers.com

Kist The Elphinstone Institute University of Aberdeen

PulseNet Pathogens – Yersinia Pestis Centers for Disease Control and Prevention

Sutyak, Katia, *Student presentation on Yersinia Pestis* (University of Connecticut)

OTHER

Aberdeen Maritime Museum permanent displays and temporary exhibition *Shipwreck*

Croly, Christopher P., *Aberdeen and Piracy 1400–1700* (notes for presentation)

Croly, Christopher P., *Aberdeen and the 1597 Witchcraft Panic* (notes for presentation)

Croly, Christopher P., *Aberdeen and the Plague* (notes for presentation)

Glenmore Forest Centre permanent display: *Kompani Linge* Norwegian Resistance and Glenmore

Piper Alpha survivor's quotation courtesy of the University of Aberdeen's *Lives in The Oil Industry Oral History Collection*

Personal memories recounted by family members and Norwegian visitors to Aberdeen and Glenmore

Scotland, Thomas, *War Surgery 1914–18* lecture (Aberdeen, October 2011 and online November 2011)

The Gordon Highlanders' Museum permanent displays and temporary exhibition *The Gordons in Iraq*